TWO
HUNDRED
YEARS *Stories of the*
Nation's Capital

TWO HUNDRED YEARS

Stories of the Nation's Capital

by Jeanne Fogle

Illustrations by Edward Fogle

VANDAMERE PRESS
a division of AB Associates

Published by Vandamere Press
A division of AB Associates
P.O. Box 5243
Arlington, Virginia
22205

Copyright 1991 by Vandamere Press

ISBN 0-918339-16-2

Library of Congress Catalog Number
90-071876

Manufactured in the United States of America. This book is set in
Palatino by Scott Photographics.

Acknowledgements

My sincerest thanks go out to a number of persons who have aided and supported me in the production of *Two Hundred Years*. First of all, Pat Berger, who so carefully edited the work, correcting grammar, rearranging sentences, and generally polishing all the rough spots. My thanks also to Larry Converse of Scott Photographics, who designed the type and is responsible for the aesthetic quality of the book. My overwhelming thanks to Art Brown, the most patient of publishers, who gave me direction, solid counsel, and inspiration.

To my brother, Edward F. Fogle, I owe a great debt of gratitude for providing all the delightful art work in the book. His talents have enhanced the book immeasurably, and his great sense of humor made working with him a true joy. I want to thank my father, George F. Fogle, who, as always, has given me his constant support. Lastly, I want to thank my husband, Tom Lyons, for all of his encouragement and for telling me, "You know, I'm your biggest fan."

Table of Contents

Developing the Dream City

Washington was established by compromise. From the beginning, the concept of a "Federal Enclave" was vague and confusing. Great frustration had overwhelmed Congress for seven years as they debated the possibility of creating a national capital city within a federal territory. The choice of site had been no simple matter. A Delaware River location was chosen first; the site was supported by the northern states which had voted against a more southern city on the Potomac River.

At the same time, the southern states had voted against the "northerners' bill." It was called the Assumption Act and stated that the states' debts which had been incurred during the Revolutionary War should be assumed by the Federal Government. Secretary of State Thomas Jefferson recorded his opinion of the situation and its result, the famous Compromise of 1790. He wrote:

> This measure produced the most bitter and angry contests ever known in Congress, before or since the union of the States. Hamilton was in despair. As I

was going to the President's one day, I met him in the street. He walked me backwards and forwards before the President's door for half an hour. He painted pathetically the temper into which the legislature had been wrought . . . the danger of secession . . . I proposed to him . . . to dine with me the next day, and would invite another friend or two . . . and I thought it impossible that reasonable men, consulting together cooly, could fail, by some mutual sacrifices of opinion, to form a compromise which was to save the union . . . It was finally agreed . . . the vote should be rescinded [by the southern constituency against Hamilton's bill] . . . and Hamilton undertook to carry the other point [of establishing the capital on the Potomac].[1]

On July 17, 1790, the final vote on the Residence Act was cast. Beginning in December 1800, Congress would meet in the newly located federal capital city, later to be called "Washington." As a city, Washington was only a dream. During the first 40 years, this "city in the wilderness" blossomed very slowly. Early Washington society was established not on wealth, culture, or prestige, but on sheer devotion to a place and an ideal. Devastating fires, economic depressions, and political rantings seemed not to have dampened the spirit of those first Washingtonians.

The following two hundred years of Washington history overflow with alluring stories about the people who left their mark on our nation's capital. Those history makers include farmers, businessmen, socialites, artisans, writers, architects, builders, ambassadors, journalists, and civil servants. One wonders why they came; how they lived and interacted with the Washington citizenry; and what legacy they left behind. Some were heroes, visionaries, philanthropists, and teachers; others were hustlers, hussies, and gossip-mongers. Most inspired just a small community in their time but a few others exerted an influence felt worldwide.

Long before Congress chose the location for the new capital city, George Washington recognized the importance of the area. The Potomac River was the link to western waterways. In 1785, George Washington organized, and became president of, the Potomac Canal Company. He wrote:

No well-informed mind need be told . . . that the flanks and rear of the United territory are possessed by foreign powers, and formidable ones too; nor how necessary it is to apply the cement of interest to bind all parts of the Union together by indissoluble bonds . . . The western settlers . . . stand as it were upon a pivot. The touch of a feather would turn them any way.[2]

Commercially, George Washington identified the Potomac River site as a "gateway to the interior," with two well-established, prosperous ports: George Town and Alexandria. Militarily, he realized the importance of a permanent binding of the western territories (Ohio and beyond) to the eastern seaboard states, so that their allegiance would not be given to Spain or Great Britain.

Congress requested a 10-mile-square territory. Major Andrew Ellicott, who held the unofficial title of "geographer general of the United States," was chosen to survey the land. He hired as an assistant, his brother's neighbor, Benjamin Banneker, a man of African and English ancestries. Banneker had received a basic education as a schoolboy, but throughout his life he continued to educate himself, showing a true penchant for astronomical research. Ellicott described the area they surveyed: "This country intended for the Permanent Residence of the Congress, bears no more proportion to the country about Philadelphia . . . for either wealth or fertility, than a crane does to a stall-fed Ox!"[3]

Tremendous problems became apparent immediately. President Washington met with resistance when he began negotiations for the purchase of the land from the owners. He chose Major Pierre L'Enfant to design the city; but the three commissioners, Thomas Johnson, Daniel Carroll, and David Stuart, whom he chose to oversee the work showed no respect for L'Enfant's genius. L'Enfant showed no regard for their position. Within months, turmoil reigned over progress.

There were other obstacles to overcome in building the city. There was a lack of skilled labor, funds, and building materials. Because L'Enfant had been relieved early of his responsibilities, there was no one to guide the project. Major federal buildings were designed by architectural competitions. Private investment in property became limited to speculators; many builders went bankrupt. The majority in Congress was reluctant to support the building efforts fully since the area had been chosen by compromise.

Just months before Congress was to arrive in December 1800, then Secretary of the Treasury Oliver Wolcott, Jr., wrote: "I do not perceive how the members of Congress can possibly secure lodgings, unless they will consent to live like scholars in a college or monks in a monastery, crowded ten or twenty in one house, utterly secluded from society."[4]

Six months later, the new Secretary of the Treasury, Albert Gallatin, observed:

> Our local situation is far from being pleasant or even convenient. Around the Capitol are seven or eight boarding houses, one tailor, one shoemaker, one printer, a washing woman, a grocery shop, a pamphlets and stationery shop and an oyster house. This makes the whole of the federal City as connected with the Capitol.[5]

When Congress arrived, they were greeted by mud streets and thick forests. Men shot game in the fields near the White House; cows and pigs roamed free. The population was counted as 3,210 persons including 106 Representatives, 32 Senators, the President, four cabinet members, 131 government clerks, as well as lawyers, doctors, shipbuilders, shopkeepers, laborers, artists, servants, slaves, and U.S. Marines.

Over the next 30 years the population grew slowly by about 1,000 people a year. Private homes began to replace the forests; a few ambitious investors tried out new business ventures; and Congress returned faithfully each year, even after the British burned their Capitol in 1814. Optimism prevailed, as evidenced by Robert Sutcliff's early 19th-century observation: "We only need here houses, cellars, kitchens, scholarly men, amiable women, and a few other such trifles, to possess a perfect city. In a word, this is the best city in the world to live in—in the future."[6]

One of the first to recognize the possibilities of making a profit in the new city was the farmer, **Davey Burnes**, commonly called "Crusty Davey." George Washington called him

Davey Burnes' Cottage

"the obstinate Mr. Burnes." His name is mentioned more frequently than any other original proprietor of the land that would become Washington, D.C.

By all accounts he was considered stubborn, impertinent, "a constant source of trouble," and in possession of an "unyielding disposition." "A very bigoted, choleric Scotchman, fond of controversy, and never known to agree with any one in the slightest particular . . . a coarse, illiterate planter of a surly disposition, and hard, obstinate, and selfish in his dealings with his fellows."[7]

He owned a large portion of the land upon which the executive mansion was to be built. Perhaps he did not want to sell, or he did not want the government moving onto his land. Perhaps he was holding out for the highest price, or he just enjoyed driving a hard bargain. For whatever reason, he resisted all of President Washington's attempts to explain the advantages he would gain through the transfer of his land to the government in 1791. Washington is said to have lost all patience. One account states that Washington told Mr. Burnes, "Had not the Federal City been laid out here, you would have died a poor tobacco planter!" To which Davey Burnes was said to reply, "I suppose, Mr. Washington, you think people are going to take every grist from you as pure grain; but what would you have been if you hadn't married the rich widow Custis! . . . a land surveyor . . . an' a mighty poor one at that."[8]

Ultimately, Davey Burnes did transfer the necessary land, and he received the highest price per acre paid by the government. All through the 1790s, he continued to grow tobacco in his fields, which occupied prime land in the northwest quadrant of the city (all the land bounded by 3rd Street, H Street, 18th Street, and Constitution Avenue, Northwest.) He was known to complain bitterly about damage to his crops when Pennsylvania Avenue was cut through his land, and he complained all the more about damage to his land caused by the construction of the White House nearby.

Davey could not be persuaded to move from his old home. It is said that one of the conditions he demanded from the government, when he transferred his land, was that "the modest house in which he lived should not be interfered with in the laying out the city." The cottage was frame, one and one-half stories high, with two rooms on the ground floor. It resembled the huts lived in by slaves. It stood on the property which Davey Burnes' grandfather, David Burnes, had purchased in 1721; Davey inherited the property from his father, James, in 1772.

In 1799, Davey Burnes died, a year and a half before the arrival of Congress. His reputation lived on for another 100 years. His cottage stood until 1894; it was the oldest existing building in the city at the time. Saving Burnes' cottage from destruction was one of the first popular attempts at historic preservation in Washington. Burnes' daughter, Marcia, had taken pains to preserve the structure during her lifetime. She was as sweet a person as her father was impertinent. She was 17 years old when she became the sole inheritor of his extensive real estate holdings, valued at more than $1.5 million. Realizing that his legacy would live on through her, Davey's last words to his daughter were said to have been: "Marcia, you have been a good daughter; you'll now be the richest girl in America."[9]

Marcia Burnes Van Ness, became known by the unofficial title "the heiress of Washington City." She was the first of a long line of Washington belles: "She was perhaps more talked of than any other female in the District of Columbia at that time, about 1798 . . . many young men were desirous of making her acquaintance, but most of them lacked the courage."[10]

At the age of 14 years, Marcia was sent to Baltimore by her father, Davey Burnes, where she received an excellent social and literary education. Upon her return to Washington in the late 1790s, it was recorded that:

> Troops of gallants began to seek the favor of the beautiful heiress. The wooers were generally treated with cutting remarks from [her father] Davey Burnes, and promptly shown the door . . . [they] saw Marcia as a splendid matrimonial prize . . . [a few] craftily allowed the old Scotchman to win their gold at cards, and awakened good feelings by generous gifts of mellow usquebaugh [a strong whiskey cordial flavored with spices].[11]

Three years after her father died, she fell in love with John Peter Van Ness. John was the dashing, brilliant, freshman Congressman from New York, described as "well-fed, well-bred, and well-read." He arrived in Washington in January 1802. Six months later they were married on Marcia's 20th birthday, and together they became the favorites of early Washington society. A month after the wedding, he received an appointment as major in the District Militia from Thomas Jefferson. When he returned to Congress the next fall, his political enemies succeeded in having him expelled on a technical violation of the Constitution that prohibits holding two positions simultaneously in the U.S. government. Rather than offering to resign the honorary position in the militia, he let his marriage determine his future. He gave up his political career in Congress and became a permanent resident of Washington.

The couple gave grand entertainments at the home designed for them by the brilliant architect Benjamin H. Latrobe. It was said that ". . . the proceeds of many a city lot vanished in high living."[12]

Both Marcia and John became leaders in the community and did a great deal to advance the prosperity of Washington. John served as president of both the Bank of the Metropolis and the Washington branch of the U.S. Bank (the largest financial institution in the country at the time). He continued to serve in the District militia, attaining the rank of general. He was a promoter and supporter of the Washington Canal, the Washington Monument Society, the Volunteer Fire Department, and the local theater. He served as vestryman at St. John's Church on Lafayette Square, and became the mayor of Washington in 1830.

Sorrow filled their later lives when their only daughter, Ann Elbertina, died in childbirth just two years after her marriage to Arthur Middleton of South Carolina. The grandchild later died of fever. After these losses, Marcia devoted her life to charitable works. She gave land for establishment of the Church of the Ascension as well as for the Washington City Female Orphan Asylum, of which she was a founder and superintendent.

Van Ness Mausoleum

In 1832, an Asiatic cholera epidemic scourged the country. Marcia dedicated her time to nursing those afflicted in Washington. She herself fell victim to the cholera and died on September 9th of that year. The next day, Congress, then in full session, adjourned to pay tribute to Marcia Burnes Van Ness. She is the only woman to be so honored by Congress.

The grief-stricken John Van Ness hired George Hadfield to construct a tomb at tremendous expense when his wife passed away. Hadfield designed it after the Temple of Vesta in Rome. The touching sentiments to Marcia inscribed on the tomb wall, though now barely legible, serve in one small way to preserve the memory of this once popular Washington couple:

> She whom the poor deplore, the good revered;
> The wise admir'd and the vicious fear'd;
> In whom sense, sweetness and accomplishment
> New charms to dignity and virtue lend.
> Is gone—but shall we doubt the Almight's love?
> Is not all earth below; all Heaven above?
> And thou her partner! sunk in grief,—thy own
> Be hushed, since bursts from every heart a groan
> Though struck down thus by thunder of the skies
> When sympathy like this supports you—rise![13]

John Van Ness lived on in the mansion for another 14 years. When he died, the property passed to collateral heirs. The last acre of property passed out of their possession in 1875. Today, the old carriage house designed by Benjamin Latrobe in 1813, at 18th and C Streets, Northwest, the Van Ness mausoleum in Oak Hill Cemetery, and Van Ness Street, in northwest Washington are all that remain of this once great family.

Washington itself is the legacy of **Pierre Charles L'Enfant**. When L'Enfant left France for America in 1777 to join the Continental Army, he was just 23 years old. Because of his engineering background, he was commissioned a captain in the Corps of Engineers. Though seriously wounded while participating in the assault on Savannah, he continued to serve. When he was taken prisoner at the siege of Charleston in 1781, Rochambeau negotiated his release. After his release from prison, he was brought to the attention of George Washington who wrote, "Your zeal and active services, are such as reflect the highest honor and are extremely pleasing to me, and I have no doubt they will have their due weight with Congress in any future promotion in your corps."[14]

In the following year L'Enfant was promoted to major in the Corps of Engineers. "A man of many accomplishments, with an overflow of ideas and few competitors he was the factotum of the new nation."[15] L'Enfant gained a popular reputation as a gifted artist during the war by sketching pencil portraits of his fellow officers. At Lafayette's request, even General Washington had his likeness sketched by "Monsieur Lanfang" (as Washington pronounced his name). No one seemed better qualified, after the war, than L'Enfant to design the insignia for the newly established Society of the Cincinnati. This organization was founded by commissioned officers who served in the regular American Army or Navy during the Revolution.

After Congress left Philadelphia in a huff and met in New York, they needed proper accommodations. L'Enfant was asked to remodel City Hall in New York, which he did with great finesse. Incorporated into the architectural design for the first time were typical American motifs: stars and stripes, medallions embossed with the symbol *U.S.*, and an eagle with 13 arrows in its talons. The eagle became the most talked about of all the motifs.

Having heard of Congress' plans to create a federal city, L'Enfant wrote President Washington in 1789:

> . . . Your Excellency will not be surprised that my ambition and the desire I have of becoming a useful citizen should lead me to wish to share in the undertaking [of designing the capital city] . . . No nation had ever before them the opportunity offered them of deliberately deciding on the spot where their Capital City should be fixed . . . And although the means now within the power of the country are not such as to pursue the design to any great extent, it will be obvious that the plan should be drawn on such a

scale as to leave room for that aggrandizement and embel-
lishment which the increase of the wealth of the nation will
permit it to pursue at any period however remote.[16]

Washington reasoned that he knew no one better qualified,
and welcomed L'Enfant and his unique quality of visualizing
en grande. With unfettered energy, L'Enfant embraced this
great commission. Everything he planned, he devised with
an intention; he found the *raison d'etre* for every detail. L'Enfant wrote:

> After much menutial [sic] search for an eligible situation,
> prompted, as I may say, from fear of being prejudiced in
> favor of a first opinion, I could discover no one so advan-
> tageously to greet the congressional building as is that on
> the west end of Jenkins heights, which stands as a pedestal
> waiting for a monument.[17]

L'Enfant carefully chose the site for the President's Palace.
He visualized noble buildings and handsome monuments lining "the grand avenue connecting both the Palace and the
Federal House."[18] His plan included a temple for national
semireligious celebrations and a pantheon for the illustrious
dead. He thoughtfully placed public buildings with reference
to their surroundings; and he devised a picturesque and attractive arrangement of thoroughfares varied with gardens,
parks, and fountains. He reveled in detail. The squares were
to be allotted, one to each of the states forming the Union.
L'Enfant continued:

> The centre of each square will admit of statues, columns,
> obelisks, or any other ornament . . . to perpetuate not only
> the memory of such individuals whose counsels or military
> achievements were conspicuous in giving liberty and inde-
> pendence to this country, but also those whose usefulness
> hath rendered them worth of general imitation, to invite the
> youth of succeeding generations to tread in the paths of
> those sages or heroes whom their country has thought
> proper to celebrate.[19]

At the crossing of the parks south of the President's Palace
and west of the Congress' House (where the Washington

Monument now stands), L'Enfant planned a site for the equestrian figure of George Washington. Most importantly, he wrote, the plan ". . . must leave to posterity a grand idea of the patriotic interest which promoted it."[20]

The future defense of the United States was a major concern to L'Enfant. "How and upon what foundations could it be supposed that America will have nothing to fear from a rupture between any of the European Powers?" wrote L'Enfant. "A neutral power must be ready for war, and his trade depends on the means of protecting and making his colors respected."[21]

Only a genius could have created the design of a whole city in 11 months and 3 weeks. L'Enfant's plan is as viable today as it was 200 years ago. Some authorities suggest that L'Enfant modeled the new city after Versailles. Many analogies have been drawn, but none so fascinating as the similarities between the Versailles' hunting forest and Washington's street pattern. The traditional French *chasse a courre* (mounted hunt) required a specially landscaped forest. The paths consisted of a checkerboard grid of roads overlapped by a diagonally slanted grid of paths. The diagonals allowed the hunter to move quickly through the forest. The intersections created by the crossing of the diagonals and squares were called *ronds* or listening points. When the hunter needed to locate his hounds, he went to a *rond*, where the roads branched out in all directions, and watched his horse's ears as they pricked up in the direction of the hunt.

The placement of the Palace of Versailles can be compared on a map to the placement of the Capitol. L'Enfant might have enjoyed the concept of the seat of power no longer being in the absolute monarch, but with the people. The city of Versailles extends to the east, with three great avenues radiating from it. L'Enfant turned the facade of the Capitol to the east with three avenues radiating from it in a similar manner: East Capitol Street, Pennsylvania Avenue, Northeast and Maryland Avenue, Southeast. The White House is the second focal point. It was placed in relation to the Capitol in the same way the Trianon is to the Palace of Versailles. The White House and the Capitol are formally connected, not by

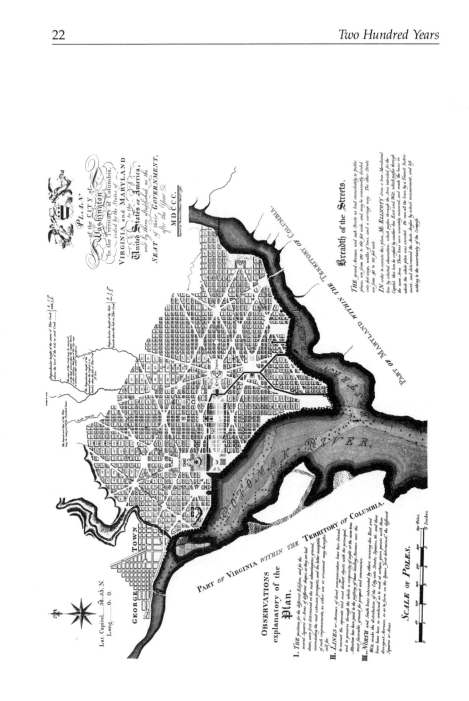

L'Enfant's Plan

Pennsylvania Avenue, but by the two parks L'Enfant designed south of the White House, and west of the Capitol. This design corresponded to the Versailles' connecting gardens and pools.

Forever temperamental, L'Enfant was soon at odds with anyone who did not comprehend his vision for the city. His first major standoff was with the owner of the land on Capitol Hill, Daniel Carroll. Carroll had begun building his new house on the square bounded by E and F Streets, 2nd Street, and New Jersey Avenue, Southeast. When L'Enfant laid out the line of New Jersey Avenue, Carroll's house was found to extend seven feet into the street. President Washington wrote to both L'Enfant and Carroll, suggesting the house could be moved at no expense to the owner or allowed to stand for six years, then removed without compensation. Before Washington's letters reached their destination, however, L'Enfant instructed his assistants Isaac Roberdeau and Benjamin Ellicott to pull down the walls. The commissioners appointed to oversee L'Enfant's work demanded his resignation. One of the commissioners was Daniel Carroll's uncle. L'Enfant tried to explain:

> . . . [regarding] the peculiar circumstances attending the undertaking of Mr. Carroll of Duddington . . . I acted with propriety on proceeding as I have done . . . I wrote him twice stating the circumstances and obligation I was under as charged with the execution of the plan to proceed to the demolishing of the house in case he should decline or delay availing himself of the alternative I offered him to effect this himself . . . It was necessary and expedient that the measure should be proceeded to with alacrity. It was proper— as I proceeded to it of right and with as much confidence as in directing a tree to be cut down or a rock to be removed where obstructive to the operation or impediments in the streets.[22]

Washington wanted to avoid a scandal. He wrote that it would be a serious misfortune to remove L'Enfant. "I know not where another is to be found who could supply his place."[23]

More problems arose with the engraving of the city's plan necessary for the sale of lots to raise money to build the public buildings. L'Enfant said he gave a copy to the engraver, but he wanted to add more details before it was printed. The engraver explained he had no copper for the plate and that the copy of the plan was inadequate for an engraving. Andrew Ellicott, who had worked with L'Enfant while surveying the original 10-mile-square Territory of Columbia, was then asked to prepare the plan to be engraved, using L'Enfant's work, which he did, to L'Enfant's horror. ". . . to my great surprise it now is, unmercifully spoiled and altered from the original plan to a degree indeed evidently tending to disgrace me."[24]

The commissioners and L'Enfant battled over everything until he gave an ultimatum to George Washington: dismiss the commissioners or allow him to act independently. The commissioners responded by demanding his removal. In the end, Washington agreed with the commissioners and Secretary of State Thomas Jefferson, who in 1791 wrote:

> It having been found impracticable to employ Major L'Enfant, in the degree of subordination which was lawful and proper, he has been notified that his services are at an end. It is proper that he should receive that reward of his past services, and the wish that he should have no just cause of discontent suggests that it should be liberal. The President thinks of $2,500 or $3,000, but leaves the determination to you.[25]

The commissioners took Jefferson's recommendation and made L'Enfant an offer. Upon receiving their proposal, L'Enfant replied:

> Without inquiring the principle upon which you suggest this offer, I shall only here testify my surprise thereupon, and in testimony of my intention to decline accepting of it I hasten expressing to you my wish and request that you will call back your order for the money and not take any further trouble about the lot.[26]

All but two of the local landholders (Mr. Carroll and his nephew) protested L'Enfant's dismissal. One of the newly arrived investors, Samuel Davidson, felt compelled to write to Washington:

> I Pray God to realize your hope and my fervent wish, by the return of Major L'Enfant . . . and to remove by a halter or otherways, those blockheads of Commissioners now in authority there, who do everything in their power to prevent the prosperity and establishment of that City.[27]

L'Enfant's remaining years were inconsequential. He accepted a commission in 1792 to design a great New Jersey manufacturing plant and the surrounding city, but funds proved totally inadequate. Two years later, he designed the fortifications at Mud Island on the Delaware River, which were never built. He was offered a commission as professor of engineering at the U.S. Military Academy at West Point, but he did not respond. In 1814, he was asked to remodel Fort Washington, in Maryland, but he was dismissed over certain disagreements. He was occasionally seen in the streets of Washington, ". . . a man of medium height, with a bright, intellectual face and courteous manner. He usually wore a blue frock-coat of antique fashion and bell-crowned hat."[28] He was known to haunt the committee rooms of Congress as a claimant for compensation for his services as the original designer of Washington. Benjamin Latrobe, architect of the Capitol, remembered him:

> Daily thro' the city stalks the picture of famine, L'Enfant and his dog. The plan of the city is probably his, though others claim it. It is not worth disputing about . . . He is too proud to receive any assistance, and it is very doubtful in what manner he subsists.[29]

L'Enfant's last years were spent on the Diggs family's farm in Prince George's County, Maryland. He died there in 1824 and was buried in a grave marked only by a cedar tree. Many tried over the years to transfer his remains back to the great city he designed, including philanthropist William Wilson Corcoran. It was not until April 28, 1908 that L'Enfant was finally honored.

L'Enfant was reinterred on the hill above Arlington Cemetery. The view of Washington from that spot is magnificent.

In the dedication speech on that day, a most appropriate quote was borrowed from the tomb of Sir Christopher Wren in St. Paul's Cathedral in London: *si monumentum requiris, circumspice*; that is, if a monument is required, just look around.

L'Enfant's nemesis in Washington was **Daniel Carroll of Duddington.** Carroll's life could best be described by the saying, "The unexpected always happens." He was a young man of 26 years when Congress announced a plan to move to a new capital city on the Potomac River. He was the richest and most important original proprietor of this land, and he considered himself the most favorably situated.

Unfortunately, his name is most often recalled in connection with the fight that led to the dismissal of Pierre L'Enfant. Ultimately, the government compensated Mr. Carroll who then constructed a new mansion nearby. He felt absolutely confident that the southeast quadrant of the city, where his lands were situated, would become the principal center of Washington society. He was a ". . . rather conceited, showy youth, but with a good brain and kind heart . . . [and] was ambitious to be an aristocrat after the manner of other members of the prolific Maryland family."[30]

Daniel Carroll's relatives included Charles Carroll III of Carrollton, a signer of the Declaration of Independence, who had been a remarkably successful planter, businessman, and politician. Charles Carroll was the longest lived of the signers, and the only one who was Roman Catholic. Another relative, John Carroll, was the first American archbishop and founder of Georgetown University. John's brother, also named Daniel Carroll (of Carrollton), was the uncle of Daniel Carroll of Duddington.

Business was in the younger Daniel Carroll's blood. He had a shipping company and the busiest brickyard in the new city. He soon became involved in one of the biggest building undertakings in Washington. Three land speculators from Philadelphia approached him to sell them lots on promissory notes with the understanding they would build fine houses on them with bricks from his brickyard. All the property in the area would thereby increase in value.

The plan to build as many as 20 buildings proved to be Carroll's downfall. The partnership found they were short of cash; it was ". . . so cursedly scarce that nothing will command it."[31] Labor was also hard to find. Daniel Carroll, who known to be extremely obstinate, held the men to their contract. A major push brought at least 15 buildings under cover by the specified date. The newspaper reported a great celebration in 1793 for ". . . the greatest effect of private enterprize of any in the city, and for the time in which they were building, the greatest in the U.S . . ."[32] The buildings, however, were never completed and stood in a state of ruin for many years.

Meanwhile, Daniel Carroll became president of the Columbian Turnpike Company, the Bank of Washington, and an incorporator of the Eastern Branch Bridge Company. He built the first tavern in Washington on what is now the Capitol grounds. The tavern was destroyed during the British invasion of 1814. In 1805, he built a three-story, fifty-room hotel at First and East Capitol Streets, Southeast, which became a residence of preference for congressmen. A few years later, he added two other large buildings to the hotel, and the group became known as Carroll's Row. Abraham Lincoln lived there when he was a member of the 13th Congress. The buildings were torn down in the 1880s and replaced by the Library of Congress.

Concerning the construction of his own mansion, Carroll was a free spender. He hired Benjamin Latrobe to complete it in 1797. He named it *Duddington*, after the original land grant patent, *Duddington Manor*. For more than a century this long, two-story brick house with a white colonial-style porch was a landmark in Washington. As the first real mansion built in Washington, it was the site of many lavish parties, including receptions for all the presidents from Adams to Jackson. Daniel Carroll ". . . wasted a great deal of money in entertaining dignitaries, and he lived to see the time when the sum he had often carelessly expended for a single entertainment would have saved him from severe distress."[33]

Tradition has it that Daniel Carroll kept prices of his city lots high, thereby discouraging any buyers other than speculators. In fact, however, he advertised his lots for sale on easy terms, and was the first to give mortgages and notes and to assume the obligations of those less fortunate.

Daniel Carroll, who had expected to gain fantastic wealth, died in poverty. In 1837, he wrote:

> I perfectly remember that the general opinion was that so great was the gift that the citizens never would be subject to taxation for the improvement of the streets having relinquished every alternate lot to the Government. Instead some were so wild as to suppose . . . the Government might pave the streets with ingots of gold or silver. After nearly half a century the result is now fully known: the unfortunate proprietors are generally brought to ruin and some with scarcely enough to buy daily food for their families.[34]

Although Carroll lost his fortune, he was granted longevity. He was the last of the original proprietors to die; his name will be associated forever with the early development of the city of Washington.

Another character who played an early role in Washington's development was **Sam Blodgett**. Some people remembered him as a prominent figure in the early promotion of the new city of Washington; others recalled him being "as cunning as a serpent."[35]

He called himself an adventurer while others called him a newcomer. By whatever title, he was a man of means and amongst the first to come to the nation's capital. His book, *Thoughts on the Increasing Wealth and National Economy of the United States*, was the first printed in Washington. He was the first president of the Bank of Columbia and also the first to purchase land in the new city. He bought a 494-acre tract named *Jamaica* just north of the White House in 1791 from Phillip Fendell of Alexandria. Later, he bought a number of lots throughout the city, investing an estimated $40,000.

Blodgett parlayed his way into an appointment as ". . . supervisor of the buildings and in general of the affairs of our [the Commissioners] care,"[36] or the resident official who was to serve in the commissioners' absence. The commissioners were from neighboring states and found it difficult to always

Blodgett's Hotel

be on site. The appointment lasted only one year and ended in 1793. Concerning it, President Washington wrote:

> With respect to Mr. Blodgett . . . I have not hesitated on former occasions to declare . . . from the moment his conduct began to unfold itself, that his appointment did not in my judgement answer the end which had been contemplated . . . it appears evidently enough now, that speculation has been his primary object from the beginning . . . I wish you may have seen the worst features in Mr. Blodgett's conduct . . . little confidence I fear is placed in Mr. Blodgett, and least where he is best known.[37]

This rebuke was just the beginning. Blodgett had come from New Hampshire where his father was an inventor and businessman. One year of military service during the Revolutionary War was enough for him. He resigned and went to Boston where he made significant money in East Indies trading. Next, he moved to Philadelphia and became acquainted with many of the great men who were planning the new nation's capital. After the site was chosen, and the deeds were signed over by the original land proprietors, he moved to Washington and began a career in land speculation.

Blodgett's great scheme for promoting Washington turned out to ruin him, but not before it became one of the greatest sources of trouble to all those associated with promoting Washington. His idea for a lottery to help the sale of lots in the city was originally well sanctioned. The first prize would be a grand hotel, valued at $50,000, designed by James Hoban, architect of the White House. A central location was chosen between the Capitol and the White House up on the E Street ridge at 8th Street, Northwest. A grand Masonic ceremony and huge party accompanied the cornerstone laying.

The drawing for this grand hotel was planned for the fall of 1793 after the sale of 50,000 tickets at $8 each. The drawing did not begin, however, until a group of businessmen formed a company to purchase all the unsold tickets. It was to last for more than a year. In the interim, Federal Lottery No. 2 was started. The name was intended to give the illusion of official sanction, but in fact it was another of Blodgett's personal ventures. The first prize was to be a great house valued at $30,000, with lesser houses offered as other prizes. Again the drawings proceeded with such slowness that the *Washington Gazette* suggested in an editorial that it might be ". . . ten years before the drawing was completed . . . [and] all those holding tickets were advised to mention them in their wills."[38]

In 1794, construction of the grand hotel was begun but it was not completed until after the turn of the century. The building never was used as a hotel. It was a two-story structure with an attic and basement, 120 feet wide, with a classical pediment adorning the entrance. It must have been an imposing mass in the fields and woods of Washington. By this time all responsibility for payment on all lottery prizes had been assigned solely to Samuel Blodgett. An early visitor to Washington, the Duke de la Rochefoucauld-Liancourt, expressed a generally held supposition that Blodgett had reaped a large profit from this. He suggested that Blodgett was probably the only man not deceived in the transaction.

The winning ticket was held by Robert S. Bickley of Philadelphia, who admitted to paying $3 over the asking price, giving vent to the speculative atmosphere under which the tickets had been sold. Since the hotel was uncompleted, however, Bickley filed a suit against Blodgett in 1798, and in 1802, a judgment was entered against Blodgett. Bickley was given the hotel, such as it was, and an additional payment of $21,500, a sum determined to be the difference between the stated and real value of the structure. All of Blodgett's property was deeded over to Bickley, who immediately sold as much of it as he could.

The general impression at the time was that Blodgett had mismanaged the lottery and that he was unscrupulous or dishonest. No record exists to substantiate this. He was a man with money, enthusiasm, and great ideas, but who, it was said, ". . . was not fitted to handle practical affairs."[39] There was never evidence of fraud.

In 1798, Blodgett, still possessing a strong sense of humor, wrote to his dear friend, the architect Dr. William Thornton.

These two men had become close associates with similar views and a shared sense of curiosity surrounding all matters of intellectual pursuit. Blodgett wrote:

> There was never a lottery in this country for more than half the amount [of the ones he held in Washington]. No, sir, although you understand the building of federal cities, capitols, anatomy, painting, botany, and the belle lettres, and such trifles give no leave to assure you that you are not yet sufficiently instructed in the more noble and more exalted science of lottery making.[40]

When Blodgett was thrown in prison, Thornton gave a $10,000 bond to allow Blodgett ". . . the liberty to walk therein, out of the prison, for the preservation of his health."[41] He walked beyond the limits, and when he failed to return, Thornton was held responsible for full payment of the bond which he could hardly afford. Blodgett did reappear eventually and began soliciting subscriptions for a national university, and a monument to General Washington. Even from his prison cell, he continued these solicitations.

A forgotten figure, Samuel Blodgett died in a Baltimore hospital in 1814. No notice was given of his death in the local newspapers. In 1819, however, the fund he had started for a national university was discovered. The fund amounted to $7,000, which had doubled with interest over time. His lottery-sponsored hotel building, sometimes called the Grand Hotel, or the Union Pacific Hotel, was best remembered as Blodgett's Hotel. It was the site of the first major entertainment in the city, a theatrical production in August 1800. Later, the government bought the hotel; it was used for 30 years by the Post Office, the Patent Office, and after the British burned the Capitol, by Congress for a brief period.

After his death, Blodgett's widow pressed a legal case against those who had purchased Blodgett's property from Bickley. She stated that the owners were ". . . liable to the claim of the dower."[42] The government, owner of Blodgett's hotel, in fact, did agree to settle out of court and paid her $333.33 yearly for life. Although the hotel burned in 1837, Samuel Blodgett's name has survived through the centuries.

The man who is credited with creating some of the most beautiful buildings in Washington is Sam Blodgett's friend, **Dr. William Thornton**. He and his wife, **Anna Maria Thornton**, became one of the most popular couples in the city in the early part of the 19th century. Dr. Thornton was a complete antidote to dullness. He was a man of infinite humor, humane and generous. Although he was trained as a physician, he was called the gentleman architect of Washington. He was the man who designed the Capitol.

Dr. Thornton was a man of independent means. Born in Tortola, West Indies, he was left a significant amount of money and property by his father, an Englishman who died when William Thornton was two years old. He was educated in England and received a degree in medicine from the University of Edinburgh. Rumor has it that the degree was granted in Scotland with the understanding that he never practice there.

During his first visit to the United States in 1787, Thornton became a citizen. His interest in the application of steam power induced him to became the chief proprietor of James Fitch & Company, formed to promote Fitch's new invention, the steamboat. Later Thornton complained that, although their steamboat rivaled Fulton's, their funds and patronage did not.

In Philadelphia during the late 1780s, Dr. Thornton traveled in the best social circles. His friend, Benjamin Franklin, encouraged Thornton to exercise his architectural talents in a competition for the design of a building to house the Philadelphia Library Company. Dr. Thornton recorded in his diary, "I saw a publication for the plan of a public library in Philadelphia offering a premium for the best. When I traveled I never thought of architecture, but I got some books and worked a few days, then gave a plan in the ancient Ionic order, which carried the day."[43]

Dr. Thornton's plan was judged the best; his prize was a share of stock in the Philadelphia Library Company worth approximately $40. He also won the heart and hand of Anna Maria Brodeau, described at the time by her mother as merely a child. The newly married couple returned to Dr. Thornton's home in Tortola, West Indies, with every intention of staying. Dr. Thornton then heard of another architectural competition which captured his imagination, and he began his plans to design the Capitol of the United States. He wrote:

> The president and secretary of state published a premium of a gold medal of $500 and a lot for a house in the city of Washington for the best plan and elevation of a capitol of the United States. I lamented not having studied architecture, and resolved to attempt the grand undertaking and study at the same time. I studied some months and worked almost night and day, but I found I was opposed by regular architects from France and various other countries.[44]

Although the official competition had ended, no design had been chosen when Dr. Thornton wrote requesting permission to submit his plan late. When permission was granted, he returned to Philadelphia with his design, later named the Tortola Scheme because he conceived of it while still living in Tortola, West Indies. Almost immediately, however, he realized it was entirely inadequate. Thornton knew he would need Secretary of State Thomas Jefferson's approval, since Jefferson was considered the best-qualified judge of classical architecture in the 1790s. Thornton quickly revised his plan to satisfy Jefferson's admiration for Roman architecture. His winning design reveals a massive central section resembling the Pantheon with a pedimented entrance portico in front of a low dome. Six low, stepped rings, just like those on the Pantheon, were drawn around the dome. Thornton added two wings to the building and gave them a delicate surface decorated with pilasters and classical details.

Upon seeing the plan, Jefferson wrote, ". . . [it] had captivated the eyes and judgement of all." Although President Washington ". . . profess[ed] to have no knowledge of Architecture," he commented on its ". . . grandeur, simplicity and convenience."[45]

Dr. and Mrs. Thornton, together with her mother, made Washington their home in 1793. Within a year, Dr. Thornton was appointed the District Commissioner of Federal Buildings. He was successful in having the supervising architect of the Capitol, Etienne Hallet, discharged after he ". . . had the boldness or the foolishness"[46] to alter the Capitol plans to be his own.

The new architectural responsibilities seemed endless for Dr. Thornton. He drafted city houses for George Washington, Daniel Carroll, and others. He laid out the grounds around the White House and planned a cathedral in Baltimore for Bishop Carroll.

The most unique and original example of domestic architecture in Washington was the Octagon House designed by Dr. Thornton for John Tayloe, one of the wealthiest men in Virginia. Its novel shape conforms to the acute angle of the lot created by two intersecting streets. Technically, it is hexagonal with a large projecting semicircular bay, which must be counted as three walls to justify the name.

One of the most important dwellings in Georgetown was another of Dr. Thornton's creations. It was designed for President Washington's adopted granddaughter. Tudor Place was built of brick that was stuccoed over. The central circular entrance is unique in that it lies half within the house; its hemispherical roof is supported by slender Tuscan columns. Dr. Thornton also consulted with another of George Washington's granddaughters on the design of her home at Woodlawn. St. John's, the first Episcopal Church in Georgetown, is also his design in part.

Next to architecture, Dr. Thornton loved horses the best. He established the first race course in the city in 1801, and kept his 23 horses on his nearby farm. His fondness for racehorses was shared by John Tayloe. Many other early Washingtonians enjoyed the races, including President John Quincy Adams, who walked several miles from the White House to the course to attend a race.

Dr. Thornton became a hero in 1814. When the British burned Washington's federal buildings, he resolved to try to discourage them. As Superintendent of the Patent Office (a position he held most of the rest of his life), he persuaded the British to let the Patent Office stand by explaining: ". . . to burn what would be useful to all mankind, would be as barbarous as formerly to burn the Alexandrian Library, for which the Turks have since been condemned by all enlightened nations."[47] By this act, he saved hundreds of patent models, the Patent Office, and the Post Office. Together, these were located in Blodgett's Hotel.

A man of many talents, Dr. Thornton was highly respected by his wife, who noted her sentiments about her husband in her diary:

> His search after knowledge was perhaps too general, as it embraced almost every subject . . . he cou'd have attained perfection in any art or science had he given up his mind solely to one pursuit—philosophy, politics, Finance, astronomy, medicine, Botany, Poetry, painting, religion, agriculture, in short, all subjects by turns occupied his active and indefatigable mind.[48]

Anna Maria Brodeau Thornton began keeping a diary on January 1, 1800. It is one of a very few sources that accurately recorded early 19th-century Washington lifestyles. In her diary she wrote:

> . . . thence to the Capitol, where we staid for some time . . . while Dr. T. laid out an Oval round which is to be the communication to the Gallery of the Senate Room . . . After breakfast we walked to the ground behind the President's House which he is going to have enclosed and laid out for a garden. It is at present in great confusion, having on it old brick kilns, pits to contain water used by the brick makers, rubbish, etc . . . After dinner we walked to take a look at Mr. Tayloe's house which begins to make a handsome appearance . . . Dr. T. worked all day on the East Elevation of the Capitol. I assisted a little till evening . . ."[49]

Anna Maria also recorded the first meeting of the citizens of Washington at Rhodes Tavern where they decided on the proper observance of February 22 as a memorial day in order to pay tribute to President Washington. She made notes about the first theater performance in Washington, and she wrote of the first open-air concert on August 21, 1801, by the U.S. Marine Band ". . . which was playing at the tents which are fixed on the ground intended for an University (on E Street, between 23rd and 25th Streets, Northwest)."[50] Anna Maria wrote about small events: ". . . bought a wooden tray of a Negro Man, who has purchased his freedom by making them and bowls at his leisure."[51] She also wrote of great occasions:

> . . . the president has arrived . . . [he] came bye about three o'clock, Dr. T. had a horse got ready, and with some other gentlemen accompanied him to the Capitol. He stopt first at his house and the Treasury Office. He travels in a Chariot & four, and is going to Lodge at Tunnicliff's Tavern on the Capitol Hill. . . .[52]

It was not until after the deaths of Dr. and Mrs. Thornton, however, that it become known that Anna Maria was the unfortunate daughter of Dr. Dodd of London, who had been executed for forgery in 1777. This was a much-publicized scandal at the time. Mrs. Dodd emigrated to Philadelphia with her infant daughter and used the name of Brodeau. Her mother ran a well-respected Philadelphia boarding school. Anna Maria was accomplished in music, painting, and French. She was well-read and quite intelligent, and often at her husband's side to help him with his work.

Dr. Thornton and his wife gave more to the city of Washington than perhaps any other couple. All of his major buildings still stand in good repair as a memorial to his talent. Mrs. Thornton's diary has survived as a testimony to her competence as an observer and chronicler of her time. Both found their final resting places in Washington's Congressional Cemetery, where Dr. Thornton was honored by burial beneath one of the great sandstone cenotaphs designed by architect Benjamin Latrobe for illustrious members of Congress who died in office.

One of the most highly regarded women in Washington's 200-year history is the incomparable **Dolly Madison**. She was called the First Lady of Washington society, the new lady of the new century, the most successful social leader Washington has ever known, a social heroine, the social arbitrator, and simply, the queen. "She was all dignity and grace and affability . . . one of the happiest of human beings,"[53] wrote Margaret Bayard Smith. "Mrs. Madison is a fine, portly, buxom dame," wrote Washington Irving in 1811 when they met for

Octagon House

the first time, "who has a smile and a pleasant word for everybody."[54]

Dolly Madison was one of nine children born to her sober Virginia Quaker parents. She was educated in Philadelphia and married her first husband, Quaker lawyer James Todd, in 1790. He died in the yellow fever epidemic of 1793. Dolly and her young son, Payne Todd, moved into her mother's Philadelphia boarding house. There she met James Madison, a boarder, who was 17 years older than she. Within a year they were married. Because Madison was not a Quaker, however, Dolly was expelled by her church. When she left Philadelphia to come to Washington, she left behind her plain, grey Quaker garments lifestyle.

Washington society admired Dolly Madison. She seemed to have a near-perfect memory for names and faces, and a remarkable ability to put people at ease. She became a fashionable trend-setter; both her clothes and her menus were copied. The turban she wore became the official headdress for ladies. She revived formal receptions, elegant dinner parties, and weekly levees (fashionable little parties); her clothes were often the talk of the day. Margaret Bayard Smith, on New Year's Day, 1813, noted:

> Mrs. Madison received in a robe of pink satin and velvet, trimmed elaborately with ermine, gold chains and clasps about her waist and wrists, and upon her head a white satin turban with a crescent in front and crowned with nodding ostrich plumes.[55]

A year and a half later, on August 23, 1814, her life changed drastically when the British invaded Washington. She resolved to remain at the White House until the last possible moment. In a letter to her sister, originally recorded in her diary, she wrote:

> Dear Sister—My husband left me yesterday morning to join General Winder. He inquired anxiously whether I had courage to remain in the Presidential house till his return, and on my assurance that I had no fear but for him and the success of our army, he left me, beseeching me to take care of myself and of the Cabinet papers, public and private. I have since received two dispatches from him, written in

pencil. The last is alarming, because he desires that I should be ready at a moment's notice to enter my carriage and leave the city; that the enemy seemed stronger than had been reported, and that it might happen that they would reach the city with intention to destroy it . . . I am accordingly ready. I have pressed as many Cabinet papers into trunks as to fill one carriage. I am determined not to go myself until I see Mr. Madison safe, and he can accompany me, as I hear of much hostility towards him . . . Disaffection stalks around us . . . My friends are all gone; even Colonel C., with his hundred men, who were stationed as a guard in this enclosure. French John (a faithful servant), with his usual activity and resolution, offers to spike the cannon at the gate, and to lay a train of powder which would blow up the British should they enter the house. To the last proposition I positively object, without being able, however, to make him understand why all advantage in war may not be taken.

Wednesday morning, twelve o'clock.—Since sunrise I have been turning my spy-glass in every direction, and watching with wearied anxiety, hoping to discern the approach of my dear husband and his friends; but, alas! I can descry only groups of military wandering in all directions, as if there were a lack of arms or spirit to fight for their own firesides!

Three o'clock.—Will you believe it, my dear sister, we have had a battle or skirmish near Bladensburg, and I am still here within sound of the cannon! Two messengers, covered with dust, come to bid me flee; but I wait for him . . . At this hour a wagon has been procured; I have had it filled with the plate and most valuable portable articles belonging to the house. Whether it will reach its destination, the Bank of Maryland, or fall into the hands of the British soldiery, events must determine. Our good friend, Mr. Carroll, has come to hasten my departure, and he is in a very bad humor with me, because I insist on waiting until the large picture of General Washington is secured, and it requires to be unscrewed from the wall. This process was found too tedious for these perilous moments; I have ordered the frame to be broken and the picture taken out. It is done and the precious portrait is placed in the hands of two gentlemen of New York for safe keeping. And now, dear sister, I must leave this house, or the retreating army will make me a prisoner in it, by filling up the road I am directed to take . . . Where I shall be to-morrow I cannot tell.[56]

After the British burned down the White House, Dolly continued to preside over Washington society from the Octagon House. She set an unexcelled record for giving parties. In 1817 she moved with her husband to his Virginia estate, *Montpellier*. Rarely was their home without visitors; foreign dignitaries, prominent men, and past and present members of Congress often stopped to pay their respects. By the time James Madison died in 1836, Virginia hospitality and the excessive demands of her son, Payne (a spendthrift and a gambler), left her in near poverty. She remarked at the time, "In truth, I am dissatisfied with the location of Montpellier, when I think how happy I should be if it joined Washington when I could see always . . . my valued acquaintances of that city."[57]

In the fall of 1837, Dolly returned to Washington. She moved into the house on Lafayette Square built for her brother-in-law, Congressman Cutts, and given to James Madison in settlement of a debt. This home soon rivalled the White House as the center of Washington's social circle. Dolly was now 70 years old. Former president John Quincy Adams was the first to call on her, and he wrote about her in his diary:

> This morning I visited Mrs. Madison . . . I had not seen her since March of 1909. The depredations of time are not so perceptible in her appearance as might be expected. She is a woman of placid appearance, equable temperament, and less susceptible to the lacerations of the scourges of the world abroad than most other.[58]

At that time, it was traditional on New Year's Day for distinguished members of society to pay their respects to the President by visiting the White House. The second stop of the day, however, was always at the home of Dolly Madison. On the Fourth of July, her parlors were always filled with visitors.

Dolly's reputation as a matchmaker was also well known. She arranged the first wedding in the White House between Miss Todd, her relative by marriage, and Congressman Jackson of Virginia in 1811. She even turned her attention to the four bachelor sons of the widowed President Martin Van Buren. Dolly introduced his oldest son, Abraham, to her niece by marriage, Angelica Singleton. Within a year they were married. Angelica then served as First Lady to her father-in-law.

Maintaining Dolly Madison in a certain style became a challenge in her later years. She had very little money by 1838 when President Jackson approved an act of Congress appropriating $30,000 for the purchase of James Madison's diaries recording the debates and events surrounding the framing of the Federal Constitution. Most of this money went to pay off the debts of her son. "Upon the tongues of surviving gossipers run stories of Payne Todd's erratic life sufficient to fill a volume,"[59] stated one account. Apparently, he was genuinely fond of his mother, and she was always there to help him out. She once wrote, "My poor boy . . . forgive his eccentricities, for his heart is all right."[60]

A second Congressional appropriation of $25,000 was subsequently approved, with the support of Daniel Webster and James Buchanan, for the purchase of Madison's unpublished papers. Just before the papers were delivered, Dolly's house caught fire. True to form, she would not leave the house until these papers were safely removed from the third floor.

In one of her last appearances, July 4, 1848, Dolly attended the laying of the cornerstone for the Washington Monument. She was there, ". . . bedaubed in Pearl powder and rouge."[61] She was last seen in public in February 1849; she died on July 12 of that year. At her funeral, the pallbearers included Washington's most prominent citizens, Cabinet Members, and officers of the Army and Navy. A tremendous crowd gathered spontaneously, and marched together, accompanying Dolly's funeral procession all the way to Congressional Cemetery.

No one was more amiable or generally loved than Dolly Madison. She was *la grande dame* in manners and character. The free-speaking, uninhibited, and snuff-taking Dolly is best remembered as ". . . a lady who enjoyed every minute of living and had a faculty for passing on that enjoyment to others."

Chapter **2**

Washington Becomes a Showplace

The Jacksonian era was ushered in with an aggressive spirit in the 1830s. Partisan politics ruled the city with a power network of influential men who seized upon the opportunity to better themselves. Many hoped to receive one of the prestigious new high-ranking government positions recently made available. Faithful public servants who, for the past quarter of a century had competently worked with each succeeding administration, were suddenly left trembling, and fearful of what the future would hold. The Jacksonian newspaper, the *Telegraph* reported, ". . . no one should be continued in office who, in a country like this, cannot make an honest living"[1] when deprived of a government office. Old Washington residents were thrown into a turmoil. Several committed suicide. This was the unhappiest time yet experienced by the city's residents.

Washington society was altered forever with the arrival of a new elite. They came from Kentucky, Tennessee, and the West. A fresh assembly of New Englanders and Southerners also made their presence felt. The diplomatic corp increased as Washington became better recognized by other countries as a national capital city. There were other newcomers as never before; Irish laborers and German immigrants streamed into the city searching for work. Temperance leaders, abolitionists, native American Indians, and many others came with a cause and paraded it before Congress and the President. The sick as well as the insane poured into Washington, and one lunatic even tried to assassinate President Jackson in 1835. The *National Intelligencer* commented on the new inhabitants:

> It is a notorious fact that this city, being the seat of government, is liable to be visited by more than its proportion of insane persons, strangers who imagining that congress is omnipotent, and for the accomplishment of any wild scheme a visit to Washington (sometimes performed on foot) is all that is necessary.[2]

The decades between 1830 and 1870 proved exceptionally distressing for local commerce. It took a roller coaster ride between good times and bad. An economic depression in the early 1830s caused the failure of many businesses and all but a few banks. Although the C&O Canal was begun in 1828, construction was sluggish and it never generated a profit. The Potomac River silted and navigation was difficult. George Washington's dream for a great commercial center on the Potomac would never be realized.

Epidemics were common all during the 19th century. An exceptionally heinous cholera epidemic devastated the Washington community in 1832. The city was without a hospital, except for the infirmary in the poorhouse at 7th and M Streets, Northwest. Theaters and public entertainments were closed; the sale of fresh fruits, vegetables, and liquor was prohibited.

The Treasury Department building burned in 1833. Just two years later, the Patent Office and the Post Office (located in Blodgett's Hotel) burned as well. The necessity for constructing new, fireproof buildings became a challenge soon answered by architect Robert Mills. He is credited with creating an entirely new generation of monumental buildings in Washington. Mills also won the competition for the design of the

Washington Monument in 1832; however, his design was radically altered over the years.

Transportation across the city was getting better, even if the roads remained unimproved. Pennsylvania Avenue was the first street to be paved, but only between the Capitol and the White House. Beyond the White House, its appearance more closely resembled a cornfield rather than the great thoroughfare and principal avenue of a metropolis. Despite its deep ruts, gutters, mud, and dust, a stagecoach between Georgetown and the city was established in 1830 with twice-a-day service to the Navy Yard. By 1836, an hourly horse-drawn omnibus was introduced, along with an hourly steamship to Alexandria. Regular railroad service began to Baltimore from a makeshift station on Pennsylvania Avenue at 2nd Street, Northwest.

Washington's economic situation brightened during the 1830s. Employment opportunities improved and prospects continued to be promising for employees of the Navy Yard and for construction workers and printers. Unfortunately, the workers of Alexandria suffered since most of the local trade was diverted to Georgetown and Washington. When the situation became intolerable, Alexandria's citizens requested that the section of D.C. land that originally had been given by the state in 1790 to the federal government be given back to the state. By 1846, Congress relinquished all attachment to the 30-square-mile Virginia county (now called Arlington County), which included the city of Alexandria. From that time on, the land known as the District of Columbia consisted of the property given to the government by the state of Maryland, including Georgetown and a portion of the Potomac River.

In 1835, the attention of Washingtonians was focused on a number of landmark projects. The Treasury Department, the Post Office, and the Patent Office were all begun in that year, and construction would continue for three decades. The Naval Observatory was established in 1844. Ground was broken for the Washington Monument in 1848, and by the early 1850s, the Smithsonian Institution was becoming a reality, guided brilliantly by John Quincy Adams. The Government Hospital

for the Insane admitted its first patients in 1852 because of
the tireless efforts of Dorethea Dix. In the 1850s Montgomery
C. Meigs was designing the new aqueduct system while the
Capitol was redesigned and greatly enlarged under the leadership of architect Thomas Ustick Walter.

While all the fine physical improvements made the capital
city a more pleasant place in which to live, new, serious political problems were tearing its citizens apart. The unpleas-
antness between northerners and southerners could be felt
nowhere more strongly than Washington. Opposing opinions
and passions dominated the great congressional debates and
speeches by Daniel Webster, Henry Clay, and John C. Calhoun in the 1830s and 1850s. The abolitionist convictions expressed by Senator Charles Sumner led to his being severely
beaten with a cane on the Senate floor by Representative
Preston Brooks in 1856.

Washington, the unhurried, untidy, southern-style town,
was hurled into a world of violence filled with strangers and
an overwhelming military presence during the Civil War.
Washington's population tripled. Forts were hastily erected
in a ring around the city. Vacant city lots were transformed
into soldiers' encampments. The avenues shuddered under
the constant weight of troops, calvary, caissons, and ambu-
lances. All large structures were converted into hospitals.
Graveyards filled up, and crime flourished. Washington had
become an unreal place, and by the war's end, she was left
in ruins.

One lady who delighted in change and can be credited with
ruining the reputation of many Washingtonians is **Anne Newport Royall**. She was America's first woman journalist and
". . . the terror of politicians, and especially congressmen,"
wrote John Quincy Adams, a man she considered a close
friend. A familiar, but rarely welcome figure at social and
political gatherings in Washington, Anne Royall kept a sharp
eye on government for more than two decades. She was 60
years old when she began her journalistic career. She often
bragged: "I never had a lesson in writing having been raised
in the Wilds of the West amongst the Indians till I was grown;
I merely learned to scrawl as fancy led me."[3]

Although Anne claimed to have been kidnapped by Indians as a child, recent research indicates that the "wilds" mentioned in her writing may have only been Pennsylvania. In 1797, she married a wealthy Virginia planter, William Royall. When he died in 1813, his relatives fought for 10 years to keep her from receiving any inheritance. They established their case on grounds of adultery and won. This left Anne impoverished and destitute at the age of 54. She was, however, armed with abundant energy, a cunning imagination, and good sense of humor.

Following this difficult time, Anne Royall decided to travel across the United States, and write descriptions of the people she met and regions she saw. She became America's first woman travel writer. She produced eleven ". . . badly printed and badly written"[4] books in five years, which she sold, some in advance of publication, to pay for her trips. In her book entitled *Sketches, Life and Manners in the United States*, published in 1826, she describes Washingtonians as being characterized by ". . . ignorance, impudence and pride."[5]

Anne returned to Washington just after the publication of *Sketches*, hoping to receive a widow's pension since her husband had been a Revolutionary War veteran. She decided to make Washington her home. Within a couple of years she set up a press on Capitol Hill, hired ". . . runaway apprentices and tramping journeymen printers,"[6] and began publishing a newspaper called the *Paul Pry*.

Her feisty behavior was usually tolerated, and her mental processes amused many. Her perseverance, however, annoyed everyone. She had an inquiring mind, loved gossip, and possessed a sense of duty, as well as a volatile temper. The name of her newspaper, *Paul Pry*, suggested the character of a purveyor of idle or malicious gossip. In fact, much more than gossip filled its pages. She used it to vent her strong opinions and prejudices. Eventually she changed the name to *The Huntress*. In the newspaper's first issue she warned:

> Our course will be a straightforward one . . . we shall oppose and expose all and every species of political evil . . . We shall patronize merit of whatever country, sect or poli-

tics. We shall advocate the liberty of the Press, the liberty
of Speech, and the liberty of Conscience. The enemies of
these bulwarks of our common safety . . . shall receive no
mercy at our hands.

Let all pious Generals, Colonels and Commanders of our
army and navy who make war upon old women beware . . .
Let all pious ladies who hawk pious tracts into young gentlemen's rooms beware, and let all old bachelors and old maids
be married as soon as possible.[7]

A crusader of causes, Anne Royall became an abolitionist.
She also fought for the American Indian and was vehemently
against the evangelical churches. Imagining these churches
might come to gain control over the state, she editorialized
against Sunday schools, Sabbath observance, and church ad-
vocacy of temperance. One Presbyterian congregation
brought charges against her in the circuit court, as a common
scold. The farcical trial became a great source of amusement
for Washingtonians. She was convicted and sentenced to a
dunking. Judge Cranch, however, wisely chose not to set the
precedent in the city by using a dunking stool. Instead he
imposed a fine of $10, which other journalists volunteered to
pay for her.

Every person of any distinction who came to Washington
was paid a visit by Anne Royall and she personally solicited
subscriptions from them. She wrote kindly of those who paid
and was mercilessly abusive to those who did not. Mrs. Hugh
White, wife of a representative from New York, wrote a letter
to her sister two months after she arrived in Washington
about her first encounter with Anne Royall:

I have been dreading a visit from Mrs. Royall ever since I
came, & at last I have had it . . . [there was] a loud knock
at the door, which was soon thrown wide open by Mrs.
Hubbard, who announced, "Mrs. Anne Royall and Ladies"
. . . I gave a look at them and supposed [Mrs. Hubbard]
was playing a joke, & that she had introduced three beggar
women . . . Mrs. Royall was clad in the most common ap-
parel and very dirty—if she ever had any mind she has lost
it . . . I introduced her to Mrs. Hunt . . . [whose] face was

half a yard long & both hands were raised. I laughed till I cried. We are all expecting to come out in the next *Huntress*.[8]

The story most often told about Anne Royall is in connection with John Quincy Adams, who loved to swim in the Potomac River. On these occasions, he was accompanied to the shore by his faithful Swiss guard, in whose charge he left his clothes. Anne Royall diverted the guard and sat on Adams' garments in an attempt to interview the President. American humorists and historians loved this story, which they often retold, quoting it from Mrs. Royall's book.

John Quincy Adams later wrote of Anne Royall, "She is a virago errant in enchanted armor, redeeming herself from the cramps of poverty by the notoriety of her eccentricities, the insane fearlessness of her attacks on public characters."[9]

Although Anne Royall was never accepted by society or literary critics, she was a friend to presidents and a courageous, cantankerous old woman. She was well known by all of Washington. Her books were read by people across the country. Today they furnish an unmatched record of common life in the developing nation from the 1820s until the 1850s. Her newspapers are on file in the Library of Congress on Capitol Hill, only a block or two from where they were printed for nearly a quarter of a century.

Women are usually the targets of gossip, but in the 1850s one man stirred up more gossip in Washington than all of the ladies combined. **Baron Alexander De Bodisco** was wealthy and worldly, 52 years old, and a bachelor. "Display was the breath of life to him . . . he could do nothing without being spectacular."[10]

The baron's official title was, *His Excellency, Chamberlain of His Majesty the Emperor of all the Russians, his actual Counsellor of State, Envoy Extraordinary and Minister Plenipotentiary to the United States*. An entire entourage accompanied him to the capital city in 1837, including his servants, his footmen, his four long-tailed black horses with gilded carriage, and his two nephews, Vladmir and Boris. In order to introduce the two boys properly to Washington society, the baron hosted a great Christmas party at his new residence in Georgetown. He

© EDWARD F. FOGLE

De Bodisco House

invited all the children from the local schools; among them was 14-year-old Harriet Beall Williams.

The baron was ". . . not favored with good looks. He was old, ugly, stout, with a broad Kalmuch face, much wrinkled, prominent eyebrows and shaggy whiskers."[11] Occasionally he covered his bald head with a shiny brown wig. He was kind and well liked. Washingtonians looked upon him indulgently. When he openly displayed his affection for the young Miss Williams, however, rumors ran rampant. This romantic December-May couple was quite a curiosity. She was the tall, blond daughter of a deceased minor government clerk. She was very popular among her peers and known to be a great a tease. After school, Miss Williams and the baron were often seen walking side by side with the baron carrying Harriet's schoolbooks.

There is a story that has been often repeated about Harriet. One afternoon, she and several of her young friends were walking through Georgetown when she noticed the baron's coach approaching. She boasted to her friends, "Watch girls, I shall stop the Baron!"[12] Pretending not to have observed the advancing carriage, she strolled out into the road and stooped down to adjust her shoe. The driver pulled so frantically on the horses' reins that they reared up and jostled the startled baron. He peered from the window, only to see Harriet casually glance up, smile, and give him a wink.

They must be married, decided the baron, persuading Harriet to discuss the matter with her mother. Her family was solidly opposed to the union. Harriet confessed to the baron ". . . that her grandmother and everybody thought he was entirely too old and ugly."[13] To this, he replied that she might find someone younger and more handsome, but she would never find anyone to love her more than he did.

A great sensation was created by their marriage in April 1840. The baron ordered gowns from Paris for the bride and bridesmaids, fashioned after Russian costumes. He personally instructed Harriet's schoolgirl friends on mastering the complicated Russian wedding ceremony and conducting themselves to match the dignity of the elderly diplomats who were the groomsmen.

The groom wore a traditional blue velvet and silver Russian court costume. The bride wore white satin and silver lace, and a diamond and pearl coronet. The diplomatic corps was costumed in full regalia; the Army and Navy officers were in dress uniform. The illustrious Senator from Kentucky, Henry Clay, gave the bride away. Senator Buchanan, former emissary to the czar was among the honored guests. Others included Daniel Webster, Dolly Madison, President Van Buren, the members of the Cabinet, the Minister from the Hague, the Chevalier de Martini, and British Minister Henry Stephen Fox.

There was a grand party that evening for the immediate family and a party the next day for the guests. The President gave a party the following day for the couple. The festivities went on for two weeks. The bridesmaids were each given a ring set with their favorite stone. Among the gifts to the bride from her husband was an antique secretary desk with numerous drawers, each filled with gold and silver coins, fantastic jewels, and imported French candy. He also gave her the beautiful home in Georgetown where he had resided at 3322 O Street, Northwest.

The baron was a lavish entertainer. Each year, a Birthnight Ball was held for his wife. One young gentleman wrote a story for *Harper's Weekly* about one such party. Coming into the baron's house, the young man was greeted by regally dressed servants. As he entered the drawing room he met a ". . . fat, oily little gentleman," also regally attired, who bowed to him. He threw his cloak to the man, thinking he was a servant. A Senator pulled him back and presented him ". . . to the astonished little fellow, now struggling from under my broadcoat . . . [De Bodisco]. I had nearly smothered the Russian Minister," he recounted, "who, however, laughed merrily at the mistake."[14]

A slight dispute broke out one evening between the baron and the Mexican Prince Iturbide at the home of William Marbury. The baron was known as one of the brainiest diplomats; Iturbide was not so highly regarded. Iturbide was described as ". . . a tiny man, side whiskered, and so short he barely reached the shoulders of the ladies."[15] The altercation ended with Iturbide's calling the baron a liar. De Bodisco immediately knocked the prince down, who jumped onto a nearby sofa, bounded up and down, shouting over and over, "He knocked an Iturbide down!" The baron and the guests were duly amused.

The marriage of the old baron to young Harriet was peculiarly romantic. The pair were wonderfully happy until the baron's death some 14 years later in 1854. He had become a favorite of society, and both Houses of Congress adjourned out of respect. The President, the diplomatic corps, and Cabinet members were all in attendance at his funeral, which was marred by an unfortunate event. The pastor, who made the address, turned his ". . . narrow zeal" against the ". . . errors of the Minister's [De Bodisco] beliefs." He ended his speech by saying he trusted that ". . . the influences surrounding the closing years of his life" had altered his views, and that ". . . if he could look down upon us now he would say . . . ," and the pastor paused. De Bodisco's old friends then whispered, imitating his Russian's accent, "He would say, what a bad-managed ceremony!"[16]

More generous than most husbands, the baron told his wife that he wanted her to remarry after he was gone and make some other man just as happy as she had made him. Harriet remained in Georgetown for six years with their five children. Then she met an English captain, Gordon Douglas Scott. They were married in 1860 in a quiet ceremony in St. John's Church on Lafayette Square. President Buchanan gave the bride away and had to ". . . lead the lady slightly in advance of himself."[17] Since both the president and Harriet were full-figured persons, they had difficulty walking together down the narrow aisle. The small church was so crowded that few could see the captain standing on a hassock in order to be of equal height to his bride. They moved to India and later to England where she lived out her life.

In the 1830s, Washington gossip-mongers delighted in talking about **Peggy O'Neal Eaton**. Some people called her the most beautiful woman in America. Others labeled her "the gorgeous hussy." More than anyone else she symbolized the transition from the tempered old Washington of the 1820s into a raucous new era of the 1830s. "A blight, invisible but as ominous as an invasion of locust, fell . . ."[18] on Washington when Peggy entered society. Margaret Bayard Smith wrote about her:

> She is, it is said, irresistible and carries whatever point she sets her mind on . . . one of the most ambitious, violent, malignant, yet silly women you ever heard of . . . Mrs. Eaton's affair, at the beginning, was but a spark, but what a conflagration did it cause.[19]

Peggy O'Neal liked to brag that she was the first baby born in the nation's capital, and was just three weeks old when George Washington died. She grew up surrounded by influential people, including a number of Senators and Representatives, Vice President Clinton, Mrs. Bonapart and her son Jerome, and even the Marquis de Lafayette. They all had been boarders at Franklin House, her father's tavern. Peggy was well-educated, intelligent and witty, very attractive, flirtatious, and vivacious. She was also high-spirited, self-willed, and unconventional.

When she was 17 years old, she decided to marry a Navy purser, John B. Timberlake. He was often out to sea, and when he died 12 years later, on an island in the Mediterranean, she showed no remorse. The rumor was that he committed suicide because of a broken heart, but he probably died from an asthmatic affliction.

All during the 1820s, Timberlake was more often at sea than at home, so Peggy and her two daughters took up residence at Franklin House. Another boarder at Franklin House was the handsome Senator John Eaton. He and Peggy had often been seen together in public while Timberlake was away. When the relationship became overtly intimate, Washington society dropped her from the party invitation lists, and when she gave parties, all the ladies would send excuses why they could not come. Society began to just ignore her.

In 1828, a few months after hearing that her first husband had died, Peggy and Senator John Eaton began to make plans for their wedding on New Year's Day. All of Washington was in an uproar. Their relationship was considered scandalous and disgraceful. The ladies of Washington were aloof and indignant. One account of the day states that the ladies ". . . declare they will not go to the wedding, and if they can help it, will not let their husbands go."[20]

Society fought hard to keep Peggy out, while President Andrew Jackson fought harder to keep her in. Peggy had a true ally in the President. She and Jackson had become acquainted years before when he was a senator living at her father's boarding house. Jackson and John Eaton were also close friends. Jackson had tremendous sympathy for Peggy because his own wife, who died only weeks before he became president, had suffered terribly from malicious and unjust criticism during his campaign. Beyond that, however, he thought of John Eaton as a brother. Both Eaton and Jackson were members of the Masonic Order, as was Peggy's father. Jackson had served as a Senator from Tennessee, as did Eaton, and during their terms in office both had boarded at Franklin House.

A few months after the wedding, President Jackson was inaugurated. Members of the Cabinet and members of society started to choose sides on the issue of whether or not to tolerate President Jackson's support of socially ambitious Peggy. Margaret Bayard Smith wrote in a letter:

> Our society is in a sad state . . . to be or not to be her friend is the test of Presidential favor. Martin Van Buren [Jackson's Secretary of State] sided with her and is consequently the [President's] right hand man . . . Yet no one can deny, that the P.'s [president's] weakness originates in an amiable cause—his devoted and ardent friendship for Genl. Eaton . . . Meanwhile, the lady who caused this division, is forced notwithstanding the support and favor of such high personages, to withdraw from society. She is not received in any private parties . . . treated with marked and universal neglect and indignity.[21]

Actually Peggy was having a pretty good time, despite the fact she had been nicknamed Bellona—the Roman goddess of war. The war she presided over was a social one. When her husband was appointed to Jackson's Cabinet as Secretary of War, many prominent people objected, solely on the principle that he was married to Peggy, whom they felt was a virtueless woman.

Half of Jackson's Cabinet supported the president, and half were vehemently opposed, or at least their wives were vehemently opposed to having to socialize with Peggy. When the president gave White House dinners, he was compelled to order his Cabinet members to attend, and threatened those whose wives prohibited them from going. Vice President John C. Calhoun's wife would have nothing to do with Peggy, and therefore nothing to do with the president. Jackson soon distanced himself from Calhoun. By contrast, Martin Van Buren, a widower, stood firmly beside the president and Peggy, giving parties in her honor. This endeared him to Jackson, and years later won him Jackson's support when he ran for the presidency.

The problem in Jackson's Cabinet dragged on. The members found it difficult to agree on any issue, and Jackson completely lost control over the them. In 1831, at the suggestion of Martin Van Buren, Jackson dissolved the Cabinet. It was an unprecedented action.

Peggy called the dissolution of the Cabinet her triumph. In the end, five Cabinet members resigned; a local pastor was reassigned to Albany, New York; the Dutch foreign minister was dismissed; and Martin Van Buren was eventually elected President rather than John Calhoun. John Eaton, however, was also one of the casualties. He was removed as Secretary of War and appointed Governor of Florida. Peggy detested Florida and didn't accompany him. Later, he was appointed Minister to Spain, a position his wife thoroughly enjoyed.

Margaret and Virginia Timberlake were Peggy's two daughters by her first marriage. Margaret married a Randolph, and Virginia married the Duke de Sampayo, secretary to the French Ambassador in Washington. When Virginia and her husband died early in life, Peggy raised their children as her second family.

When John Eaton died in 1856, he left a large estate to Peggy. It included a downtown building with a store and a large hall overtop. After her husband's death, a dancing instructor, Antonio Buchignani, asked to rent it in exchange for dancing lessons for her grandchildren, who were teenagers. He was a charming young man and soon asked to move into Peggy's house. Then in 1859, he asked Peggy to marry him and she did; he was 20 years old, she was 60. Gradually, he gained control of her money, some of which he lost in bad investments. Then in 1865 Buchignani disappeared. He took not only the rest of Peggy's money, but also one of her granddaughters, who was by then a young mother of two small children. Not long afterwards, Peggy found out her errant granddaughter had given birth to another child, whose father was Buchignani.

When Antonio Buchignani returned two years later, Peggy had him thrown in jail. She agreed to freeing him only after their divorce was final, and he agreed to marry her granddaughter.

Washington continued to be Peggy's home until just days before her 80th birthday when she died. In her last years she lived alone and in poverty, however, she never lost her *joie de vivre*. A popular story of the time suggested that her last words were: "What a beautiful world to leave."

William Wilson Corcoran was a contemporary of Peggy Eaton's who chose a totally different lifestyle. He was Washington's greatest philanthropist and a native-born son, who gave his fortune to help make Washington a better place in which to live. He was a colorful, remarkably successful, prosperous, and powerful man. Considered one of the most influential figures in the capital and the nation, W.W. Corcoran was a great optimist, a believer in "Manifest Destiny," and the inevitable greatness of the United States. Son of an Irish immigrant who became a Georgetown leather merchant, Corcoran led a relatively quiet life until he was 40 years old. Having made so much money, he retired at 56 years and decided to dedicate the rest of his life to giving it away.

With George Washington Riggs, Jr., as his partner, Corcoran founded a bank in 1840 that made history; it was called the Corcoran and Riggs Bank, later known just as Riggs Bank. During the national crisis surrounding the untimely death of President Harrison in the early 1840s, the government des-

perately needed money. Corcoran became known as the
"banker statesman" when he obtained financial backing from
New York banks to help the government place a loan. A few
years later, funds were needed to finance the Mexican War.
Corcoran became the emissary between the government and
private banks. When the war bonds did not sell in the United
States, he departed on a day's notice for London. Within 10
days, he had convinced London's largest banking concerns to
purchase $5 million worth of American government bonds.
As the first sale of American securities in Europe, this event
established U.S. credit abroad.

His profits from the sales of bonds on commission were
enormous. Corcoran knew exactly what he would do first
with his new-found wealth. In the late 1840s he gave $10,000
to the city of Georgetown for the aid of the dependent population. Next, he paid off some old debts. Years before, in
1823, Corcoran and his two brothers started a business that
failed. His creditors were paid fifty cents to the dollar. Corcoran located the old creditors and paid off his debts. It was
an unheard-of gesture. He received many letters expressing
gratitude, astonishment, and sincere good wishes, such as
this:

> I have this day received from you $1,450.50, being prin-
> cipal and interest on the balance of the claim compromised
> at fifty percent, twenty years ago. This extraordinary act
> has been done by you without solicitation on my part, and
> I will take this occasion to say that, having been engaged in
> mercantile pursuits for thirty years, and during that period
> having sold upwards of $23,000,000 to various persons in
> different states of the Union, and having compromised
> claims for a very large amount, your *is the only instance* in
> which a man ever came forward after recovering his fortune,
> in the honorable manner you have done, and paid me in
> full. Be assured it will not be forgotten by me, and whenever
> occasion may occur by which I can directly or indirectly,
> serve you, it will be remembered then also.
> With my best wishes for your health and prosperity,
> Believe me, yours truly,
> T.C.Rockhill[22]

Corcoran, in 1849, bought a grand mansion on Lafayette Square, to which he added gardens and a conservatory for his art collection. It was here that he first displayed his prize sculpture, Hiram Power's masterpiece, *The Greek Slave*. This delicate nude statue was hailed in London as ". . . one work of art by an American artist that did credit to America."[23] Puritan shock over its nudity, however, caused quite a stir when Corcoran unveiled the beautiful statue, forcing Powers to explain that the figure represented ". . . the fortitude and resignation of a Christian supported by her faith in the goodness of God; leaving no room for shame." He also said the figure had been ". . . inspired by the heroic struggle of the Greek people to throw off the yoke of the Turkish masters in the war that had ended in 1830."[24] Still, when acquaintances visited Corcoran, they went separately, men, then women, to view the sculpture.

Corcoran was 35 when he married 17-year-old Louise Morris, daughter of a famous commodore. They tried to elope one evening in 1835, but they were caught by her father, who begrudgingly called a minister to his house that night so they could be properly married. Later, they had three children, two of whom died as infants. Louise herself died of tuberculosis when she was only 21 years old. Corcoran never remarried, but lavished his attention on his only surviving daughter, Louise. When she married Congressman Eustis of Louisiana, ". . . nearly 1,500 invitations were distributed the Union over."[25]

Inspired by the concept that Washington should be an intellectual and artistic center, Corcoran, in 1858, built a beautiful art gallery across from the White House, for his growing collection. Just before it was completed, the Civil War began. Because Corcoran was known to have southern sympathies, the gallery was seized by the government, as was his country estate, Harewood. He had wisely transferred his mansion, however, to the French Minister, Marquis de Montholon, so as to protect it from government seizure. One of Corcoran's friends, Senator John Slidell, became the Confederate Commissioner to France and appointed Corcoran's son-in-law to serve as his secretary. Corcoran had little choice but to leave

Corcoran Gallery of Art

the country at the outbreak of the Civil War. He was able to dispatch to Europe, however, more than $1.5 million worth of assets, which he subsequently reinvested. He spent the war years in Europe collecting more paintings and sculpture.

The end of the Civil War did not bring much happiness to Corcoran. In 1866, he went to Cannes, France, to visit his daughter, who suddenly had become very ill. She died of tuberculosis soon after his arrival. He returned to Washington, only to be "greeted" by Secretary of War Stanton, who accused him of tax evasion. The investigation was halted later, for lack of evidence.

Corcoran wanted to prove his patriotism to the nation in the 1870s. He restored his gallery and placed it under the control of a board of trustees. He contributed generously to the Washington Monument Society. He had the body of John Howard Payne, the popular author of *Home, Sweet Home*, brought back from Tunisia and given a place of honor in Oak Hill Cemetery, which he had established years earlier in memory of his wife. He also tried to honor the city's designer, Pierre L'Enfant. Corcoran wanted to bring his remains to Washington for reinterment from the humble burial grounds in Maryland or have a monument created to L'Enfant in the city. Unfortunately Congress would not support his efforts; they showed no interest in remembering L'Enfant.

Restoring the dignity of the South after the Civil War was a major concern of Corcoran's. When his friend, Robert E. Lee, died in 1880, Corcoran personally organized the memorial services. The Southern Historical Society received his liberal financial support. Travelling through the South, he made countless private gifts to those in distress. In Washington, he established the Louise Home for gentlewomen of reduced means. These ladies were primarily southern women impoverished by the war. It was said that admittance was judged by the three P's: personality, pedigree, and poverty. There is also the story, told by a streetcar conductor, of people who lined up on the sidewalk outside of Corcoran's office each morning, and to whom he would judiciously dispense "green money."

Schools and churches were often recipients of Corcoran's generous gifts. He contributed to Columbian University (now George Washington University), Maryland Agricultural College (now the University of Maryland), Washington and Lee, William and Mary, and the Virginia Military Institute. One hundred thousand dollars were set aside for the establishment of an art school attached to the Corcoran Gallery. This fund was not discovered until after his death. St. John's Church in Georgetown, the Church of the Ascension, the Episcopal Theological Seminary, the Convent and Academy of the Visitation, Washington's Roman Catholic churches, and St. Luke's Negro Episcopal Church all received "loans" from Corcoran who always tore up the paper when the loans came due.

Corcoran was Washington's most notable nonmilitary hero. A man of unusual integrity and character, and impeccable in his appearance, always wearing a red rose in his lapel. When he died in 1888, at the age of almost 90 years, it was said, "He was so much to Washington, and Washington was so much to him that the man and the city seemed indissolubly associated . . . no other name, except that which the Capital bears, no other memory except that of the Father of our Republic, are so dear to the hearts of the people of this city."[26]

The United States Congress served as the main patron of the arts throughout the 19th century. Federal buildings always needed ornamentation. One young artist who attracted the attention of Presidents, Congressmen, and Generals was the plucky, charming, and multitalented **Vinnie Ream**. Born in a log cabin in 1847, she grew up on the Wisconsin frontier where her father served as an Army mapmaker. She was encouraged to develop her artistic talents by native American Indians there who gave her paints. Her self-taught skills led her to become the first woman to receive a sculptural commission from the Unites States—at the age of 19.

When Vinnie was 14 years old, her father was transferred to Washington. In order to help with family expenses, she secured a clerkship in the main Post Office, which paid $50 a month. She was the first woman to hold such a position. While working for the government, she became reacquainted

Vinnie Ream

with Senator James Rollins from Missouri, the state of her birth. They discussed her love of art, and he introduced her to Clark Mills, a prominent sculptor working in Washington. She wrote, "As soon as I saw the sculptor handle the clay, I felt at once that I too could model and taking the clay, in a few hours I produced a medallion of an Indian chief's head."[27] Mills was impressed. Under his instruction, she began sculpting busts of congressmen, generals, and other famous clients, such as Thaddeus Stevens, George Custer, and Horace Greeley. After Vinnie finished a portrait bust of Senator John Sherman, she recorded his reaction to it and her own impressions of the events that followed:

> When he saw it, he ordered 20 or 30 to send to some of his constituents. I made first one member [of Congress], and then another, until . . . they asked me how I would like to make a bust of Lincoln—oh I was delighted. How well I remember that day when they took me up to the White House! They said, 'Here is a little Western girl, Mr. Lincoln. She is just starting out in life. She wants to model you.' He was tired, he said, of having his likenesses made; he did not know why anyone would want a likeness of him—he was so homely.[28]

Because she came from a poor background, Lincoln's sympathy was aroused. He invited her to his office during his lunch hour. For five months she worked on two different plaster model busts of the president. She finished the second one on the afternoon of April 14, 1865. She was perhaps the last civilian to speak to Lincoln before he left for Ford's Theater. In fact, Vinnie had created the last sculptural likeness of Lincoln.

In 1866 Congress awarded her a $10,000 contract to create a life-size statue of Lincoln for the Capitol Rotunda. When better-known, older male artists, like Hiram Powers, were turned down for the coveted commission, an unpleasant controversy followed. Letters of protest filled congressional offices, and newspapers across the country stated that it was indecent for a woman to be allowed to model the human figure. "These people know nothing of art,"[29] said Vinnie.

Another uproar started in Congress about her political ties. She was a supporter of Andrew Johnson, who tried to follow Lincoln's policy for reconstruction. Her compassion for those who suffered defeat in the South was well known. When Congress realized that Senator Edmund Ross of Kansas was a boarder in her parents' home, she became a target of blatant harassment. Ross' vote on the Johnson impeachment trial was very important. It would break the tie for or against impeachment of the president. Her influence was feared by members of Congress that wanted to see Johnson impeached. Her artistic career and her reputation were viciously attacked, but she stood by her convictions. Ross, in fact, did cast the deciding vote against impeachment.

Vinnie was sent to Italy in 1869 so that the Lincoln statue could be carved in carrara marble from her original plaster model. President Johnson, General Grant, Treasury Secretary McCulloch, 36 senators, and 110 representatives personally testified to her unquestionable genius. More than a year later, she returned with the finished Carrara marble Lincoln statue. While in Italy, she had become enchanted with the colorful Contidina costume of an Italian peasant. After arriving back in Washington, she created quite a stir by wearing this delightful outfit. All pettiness was soon forgotten, however, when her statue of Lincoln was unveiled in the Capitol in 1871 to deafening applause from the crowd-filled Rotunda.

When General Albert Pike admired her work, she sculpted a portrait bust for him. He, in turn, decided to instruct her in Freemasonry. Pike then conferred on her the seven Masonic degrees of "Apprentice, Companion, Mistress, Perfect Mistress, Elect, Ecossaise, and Sublime Ecossaise." Later, she received the eighth Masonic degree of "Syrene Directress of the Work," making her the first American woman to become an eighth-degree Freemason.

Vinnie Ream was visited by the wife of Admiral David G. Farragut in the early 1870s. Mrs. Farragut commissioned Vinnie to sculpt a bust of her famous husband who had just died. Vinnie, in possession of Mrs. Farragut's photographs of her husband, was granted the government contract for his statue which now stands in Washington's Farragut Square. She worked on the statue for six months in a studio at the Navy Yard.

While working at the Navy Yard throughout the 1870s, Vinnie met Army Lt. Richard Loveridge Hoxie, a wealthy engineering officer. They fell in love and were married. Afterwards he suggested that she give up her career in sculpture. She did limit her work to portrait busts for friends and allegorical statues, until she won a commission from the state of Oklahoma to sculpt a noble statue of Sequoya, the Cherokee chief, for National Statuary Hall in the Capitol. In 1906, she accepted a similar commission from the state of Iowa to create a statue of the Civil War governor, Samuel Kirkwood, for this same hall in the Capitol. Although she was not in good health, she completed the statue with the aid of some rigging and help from artist George Julian Zolnay. She is the only woman sculptor to have three major works of art inside the Capitol.

Vinnie's husband, Richard Hoxie, was a career military officer with the U.S. Corps of Engineers and an authority on fortifications. He also helped plan Washington's new streets and squares, as well as Rock Creek Park. When Vinnie died, he had a headstone designed for her and placed it in Arlington Cemetery where she is buried in the gravesite he had chosen for himself. On top of the pedestal is a bronze replica of her statue of Sapho, the poetess. On the side is a bronze plaque. George Julian Zolnay created a relief panel on the plaque on which he placed Vinnie's likeness and the phrase, "Words that would praise thee are impotent."

The creation of Arlington Cemetery can be credited to Brigadier General **Montgomery Cunningham Meigs**. He was an engineer, an architect, and a military officer. M.C. Meigs was called ". . . a competent man with an infinite capacity for detail, but imbued with an idea of his own importance."[30] M.C. Meigs was powerful; M.C. Meigs was vindictive.

M.C. Meigs was born in Georgia, schooled in Pennsylvania, and graduated fifth in his class from West Point in 1837. He served with Robert E. Lee in the Corps of Engineers, and he was closely associated with Jefferson Davis, who was President Pierce's Secretary of War. When the Civil War began, however, Meigs developed a deep hatred for Southerners who left the Union, including his own brother. They all became unpardonable traitors in Meigs' mind.

Meigs' first engineering accomplishment was the Washington Aqueduct. Jefferson Davis gave him the rank of captain in 1851 and appointed him to design a water supply system for the city. "Let our aqueduct be worthy of the nation . . . great in the name it will bear of Washington, a fitter monument to that name than obelisk or statue,"[31] wrote Meigs.

Ten years later the aqueduct was completed. Meigs had created a monument; some say it was a monument to Meigs, since he had his name stamped all over the 14 miles of stone, pipes, valves, and gatehouses. He placed Jefferson Davis' name on the Union Arch bridge in Cabin John, Maryland, which was actually the longest masonry arch in the world, supporting both a road bridge and aqueduct pipes. When the Civil War started, Meigs had Davis' name removed.

Next, Meigs was appointed supervising engineer in charge of the construction of the Capitol in the 1850s. He bullied his way past the Capitol's architect, Thomas U. Walter. For 10 years they carried on a bitter feud. Meigs wanted to create a building that was functional and efficient. He designed a massive forced-air heating and ventilation system with huge steam-driven engines to blow the air. Walter had conceived a magnificent cast-iron dome for the building, but Meigs dominated the project, as if it were his own. He even had his name cast into the iron trusses.

Meigs also was responsible for the decorative arts in the Capitol. Because he liked things showy, rich, and elaborate, he hired European-born craftsmen. One critic called the new Capitol's artwork ". . . decorative trash that would not be tolerated in a large bar saloon."[32] Walt Whitman said it was ". . . the richest and gayest and most un-American and inappropriate ornamenting he had ever seen."[33] Mark Twain called it ". . . the delirium tremens of art."[34] During this time, Meigs incurred the wrath not only of American artists, but also a number of congressmen. He tried to explain that he was shaping the Capitol ". . . in such a manner that it [would] last for ages as a creditable monument of the State of the Arts at this time in this Country."[35] In February 1861, however, he was sent to design a fort on the Dry Tortugas Islands, off the Florida Keys.

In April 1861, the Civil War broke out. Meigs was recalled and appointed quartermaster general. He was given extraordinary powers, controlling construction, supplies, and transportation for military units. One prominent Senator complained about Meigs to Secretary of War Stanton: "Mr. Secretary, I wonder how a lawyer, as you are, can keep that man Meigs where he is. Why he pays no regard to either law or justice! He is a disgrace to the army." Stanton replied, "Now, don't say a word against Meigs, he is the most useful man I have about me. True, he isn't a lawyer, and therefore he does many things that I wouldn't dare do." "Then why do you let him do them?" asked the Senator. Stanton answered, "Somebody has to do them."[36]

Meigs became a politically powerful and prominent citizen among Washington's elite in the 1870s. He befriended Seth Eastman, who taught him to sketch and paint. He befriended Joseph Henry of the Smithsonian Institution, and his successor, Secretary Spencer Baird, who encouraged Meigs' study of science.

Architecture was another of Meigs' passions. The nation's Centennial Celebration, in 1876, gave Meigs his first chance to design a building. At the end of the celebration, 34 of 40 countries who participated in the Philadelphia Centennial Exposition sent their display materials to Washington as a gift to the Smithsonian Institution. Meigs planned a brick structure 300 feet square and one story high, with a roof of iron trusses to house these display materials. The new style was called modernized romanesque and somewhat resembled a decorated train shed. The building cost of only $250,000 was phenomenally low, an amount less than the cost of the temporary structure built in Philadelphia for the U.S. exhibit. The structure today is the Smithsonian Arts and Industry Building.

The Pension Building is undoubtedly the most important structure designed by M.C. Meigs. Admirers of his work called it a major monument to the Civil War. Others labelled it, "Meigs' ugly red brick barn."[37] In 1882, construction began on the structure where eventually 1,500 clerks would be responsible for dispensing pensions to veterans of the Civil War and their families.

Meigs' model for the Pension Building was the 16th-century Palazzo Farnese in Rome. Economy dictated the building's construction in brick rather than marble; 15.5 million bricks were used. The building's courtyard space was enclosed, filled not with walls, but the largest Corinthian columns in the world. They are 75 feet tall and 25 feet in diameter. Meigs ordered the ceiling painted sky blue. Skylights and double-hung, glazed windows were installed. Forced-air ventilation took advantage of the large atrium space. Three bricks were removed from beneath each window to allow for the escape of foul air. One worker noted in winter that a peddler of wool socks and underwear could make a fortune in the Pension Building. Nevertheless, Meigs was proud of the structure and wrote, "No dark, ill ventilated corridors depreciate the health of those who work in it or depress their spirits. Every working room is lighted from windows on two sides. There is not a dark corner in the building."[38] His words did not stop the constant criticism of the building. It was branded as being ". . . an example to our national legislators of what not to do,"[39] and General Sherman supposedly commented, "The worst of it is, it is fireproof."[40]

Meigs' anti-Southern sentiment had been intense during the Civil War. He took over W.W. Corcoran's new, uncompleted Art Gallery as his headquarters, knowing Corcoran had friends in the South. When the government ran out of places to bury their dead Union soldiers, Meigs immediately chose the land around the former home of Robert E. Lee across the Potomac River from Washington. He wrote to Secretary of War Stanton in June 1864, ". . . the grounds about the Mansion [Arlington House] are admirably adapted to such a use."[41]

Stanton quickly agreed to Meigs' plan. Meigs ordered the burials to take place as quickly as possible, and near to the house. His intention was to render the mansion uninhabitable. He even had 12 bodies brought over from Washington and reinterred beside the Lees' rose garden. After the war, he requested the construction of a vault in the rose garden for the unidentifiable remains of 2,111 soldiers from nearby battlefields. His own grave is just a few hundred feet from the mansion, near that of his son who was killed in the war. The location is indicated as Section One, Lot One, in the cemetery records.

One of the European artists M.C. Meigs hired to decorate the Capitol in 1852 was **Constantino Brumidi**. He was a proud and very talented Italian gentleman who came to America as an immigrant. Almost five years from the day of his arrival in New York, he became an American citizen. He often signed his paintings, "C. Brumidi, artist. Citizen of the United States." His work has been called the most magnificent, monumental historical paintings in the United States. For more than a quarter of a century the artist labored to decorate the interior of the Capitol. He died in poverty, however, and for nearly a century he was all but forgotten.

Born in Italy on July 26, 1805, Brumidi was just a teenager when he studied at the Academy of Fine Arts and the *Academia di San Luca* in Rome. During his employment as a Papal Guard, Pope Pius IX recognized his artistic talent and gave him a commission to restore the *Loggia di Rafaello* in the Vatican. One early guide to the Capitol noted:

> When about forty years of age, Brumidi threw away his brush and his great career, declaring what he would never paint another stroke until he had found liberty. Because of an indignity suffered by a member of his family he became a revolutionary soldier and fought in vain for liberty. When almost 50 years old he was banished from Italy and came to America. Here he found liberty and became an intensely patriotic citizen.[42]

Brumidi's reputation in America spread quickly. He was invited to Washington by M.C. Meigs, who was serving as supervising engineer in charge of construction of the Capitol. Meigs was a driving force behind federally sponsored art projects. In order for "Congress to see a specimen of this the highest style of architectural decoration,"[43] Meigs suggested

EFF 7/70

Constantino Brumidi

that Brumidi execute a number of frescoes in the House
Agriculture Committee Room.

Within just a few weeks, Brumidi painted a ceiling fresco.
It was an allegorical representation of the four seasons. He
also depicted the *Calling of Cincinnatus from the Plow* and the
Calling of Putnam from the Plow to the Revolution in wall lunettes.
Then he painted a panel in the House Chamber, *Cornwallis
Sues for Cessation of Hostilities Under the Flag of Truce.* The last
work received very strong criticism. One anonymous letter
suggested Meigs' removal and the eradication of Brumidi's
work.

Despite this harsh and unreasonable criticism, and the fact
that he could have made a fortune in numerous private com-
missions, Brumidi preferred patriotism over prosperity. He
wrote, "I have no longer any desire for fame or fortune. My
one ambition and my daily prayer is that I may live long
enough to make beautiful the Capitol of the one country on
earth in which there is liberty."[44]

Brumidi was the protagonist of patriotic mural painting. His
medium was fresco, which he explained in a letter to
Congress:

> The Committee Room on Agriculture in the south wing
> of the Capitol was painted in 1855 as the first specimen of
> real fresco introduced in America. In this connection can be
> mentioned a curious mistake common in this country, and
> that is the calling all and every decoration in oil, turpentine
> or glue that is put upon dry walls, real fresco.
>
> Fresco derives its name from fresh mortar, and is the
> immediate and rapid application of mineral colors diluted
> in water, to the fresh mortar just put upon the wall,
> whereby the colors are absorbed by the mortar during its
> freshness, and repeating this process in sections day by day,
> till the entire picture will be completed. This superior
> method is much admired in the celebrated works of the old
> masters, and is proper for historical subjects or classical
> ornamentations, like the Loggia of Raphael at the Vatican.[45]

At the request of Thomas U. Walter, supervising architect
of the Capitol, Brumidi designed a fresco for the interior can-

opy of the Capitol dome. The great fresco would cover 4,664 square feet of concave space at 180 feet above the floor. The figures would have to be three times life size so that they would appear life-size from below. Brumidi suggested the cost would be $50,000, to which Walter responded:

> I am aware, as you have expressed to me in conversation that there in no picture in the world that will compare with this in magnitude and in difficulty of execution, being painted on a concave surface . . . Should you execute this work it will be the great work of your life; it will therefore be worth on your part some sacrifice to accomplish so great an achievement.[46]

Subsequently, they agreed on a lesser price. Brumidi, with one other artist, George F.W. Strieby, spent the next 11 months lying on scaffolding, creating ". . . the grandest and most imposing work ever executed." Brumidi named it the *Apotheosis of George Washington*. One book about Brumidi's art describes it:

> The fresco of Brumidi arrests the gaze as though the sky had opened and it were permitted to look into the beyond. Clouds of gold, azure rose seem hanging there spanned by a rainbow, and floating among them forms of exquisite beauty. Grand mythological figures symbolizing Force and Progress, appear there too, titanic, majestic—almost appalling with their great significance. At the center is George Washington, attended by Liberty and Victory, with the five allegorical groupings of Agriculture, Commerce, Mechanics, Marine, and Arts and Science. The most outstanding figure is Armed Liberty, trampling on tyranny, and Kingly Power. Her face is said to be that of Lola Germon.[47]

Brumidi's model for Armed Liberty, a figure in the fresco of the Capitol dome, was Lola Germon, who also had served as a model for many of his Madonna figures. They fell in love and were married when Lola was only 18 years old and Brumidi was more than 50 years old. They had one son, Laurence, who inherited some of his father's artistic talent. Lola eventually left Brumidi for a younger man, however. Their son traveled to Paris, but he was unable to make a living as an artist and returned to Washington. After his father's death, he spent his last years in St. Elizabeth's Asylum for the Insane. Brumidi also had one daughter, Elena, born to his first wife in Italy in 1842. He and Elena carried on a monthly correspondence for 27 years.

"The Brumidi decorations are second to none,"[48] wrote artist Charles Ayer Whipple. They are to be found in six Senate committee rooms, the President's Room, the Senate Reception Room, the corridors of the Senate wing, and the frieze that encircles the interior of the Capitol dome. These paintings are filled with studies of birds, butterflies, children, flowers and fruit, and with allegorical and historical portraits.

Brumidi survived the critics who called his work "abominable," "tawdry and exuberant," and "a display of gaudy inharmonious colors . . . unsuited to halls of deliberation where calm thought and unimpassioned reason are supposed to reside."[49] He rose above the attack by American artists who labeled him a foreigner. At the age of 74, a horrible accident brought an end to Brumidi's career. He slipped from the scaffolding and according to his own words in a report submitted to Congress:

> That upon the 1st day of October ult, he was engaged at work upon the Historical Painting in fresco in the Frieze of the Rotunda of the Capitol and while sitting upon a temporary scaffold and near the edge, the chair turned from under him and threw him over. He caught the round of a ladder and remained suspended by the strength of his arms for the space of fifteen minutes, till officer Lammond descended from the top of the Dome to the scaffold and called two men from the floor of the Rotunda to assist in the rescue.[50]

In a petition dictated by Brumidi just months before he died, he requested to continue working from his studio, creating the sketches and full-size cartoons with which another artist could then complete the Capitol fresco. He asked to be placed on the regular payroll, ". . . as a reward of the long life spent in the service of the government."[51]

The shock of the accident was too much for Brumidi who was then an old man. He lived only four more months. In February 1880, Brumidi died alone and in poverty at his parlor studio with his work about him. His wife had since remarried twice. His daughter remained in Rome, and no one mentioned his son's whereabouts. His life-long friend, George Strieby, paid for his burial. A site in Glenwood Cemetery became his final resting place, near the graves of his wife's parents. When he died, *The Washington Post* wrote of him:

> Constantino Brumidi, the artist, died yesterday morning at his residence, 921 G Street [Southeast], . . . Almost until the last hour he continued his work on the frescoes in the dome of the Capitol . . . It was the dream of his life that he should . . . with his own hand, lead that historic procession round the dome till the encircling frieze should be complete.[52]

Four days later, Senator Voorhees of Indiana and Senator Morrill of Vermont eulogized him in two speeches saying, "He died poor, without money enough to bury his worn-out body, but how rich the inheritance he has left to the present and succeeding ages! . . . So long had he devoted his heart and strength to this Capitol that his love and reverence for it was not surpassed by even that of Michelangelo for St. Peter's."[53]

Perhaps it was Senator's Morrill's speech, years later that inspired the writer of a guidebook of Washington to comment, "Brumidi's work so identifies him with the Capitol Building that he may almost now be called the Michelangelo of the Capitol!"[54]

Chapter **3**

A New Era

Washington is the ugliest city in the whole country,"[1] expostulated Senator Stewart of Nevada in 1870. It was dirty and overwhelmed with beggars, delinquent school-age children, and ". . . the infinite, abominable nuisance of cows, and horses, and sheep and goats, running through all the streets,"[2] noted Senator Edmunds.

Horror permeated the city when Congress gave serious thought to relocating the nation's capital. The midwestern states urged removal of the capital to the heart of the country—St. Louis. General Sherman, however, predicted that such requests would cease when the prospective residents of a new capital city realized they would have to relinquish their state citizenships and their votes.

One group of 150 influential citizens petitioned Congress in 1870, to set up a territorial government in Washington. There had been strong rumors that Congress might move from the war-torn city. An effective city government might convince them to stay. The Senate and the House, after an extended debate, passed the District Territorial Act in 1871, much to the amazement of the residents. Washington could now have an elected non-voting delegate to Congress, a council of 22 elected members (two from each of 11 wards), and a governor and board of public works appointed by the President. Federal property would remain untaxed, so the burden of all the expenses associated with the territory fell solely on private property owners.

The new territorial government proved obstreperous and was short lived. The first governor, Henry D. Cooke, stepped down after only one year. The self-assured, self-promoting "Boss" Shepherd replaced him. The Boss' comprehensive plans for improvements completely changed the face of the city in only two years, and left the city in financial ruin. In 1884 Congress pronounced the territorial government a failure and they voted it out of existence.

Tremendous new building and rebuilding projects during the late 1880s boosted Washington's economy and importance as a capital city. The National Museum was erected on the Mall in 1881. The Washington Monument was finally completed and dedicated in 1884. The great Pension Building opened in 1885. Congress appropriated funds for a new State, War, and Navy Building to be erected next to the White House. When completed in 1888, it became the world's largest office building. The Library of Congress opened in 1897 and was perceived by one newspaperman as ". . . a gorgeous and palatial monument to [America's] national sympathy and appreciation of Literature, Science, and Art."[3] Throughout the city, new schools, markets, hotels, and office buildings were erected with great zeal. Neighborhoods exploded with new rowhouses built by a population that felt secure with their weekly government wages.

New modes of transportation helped development in outlying areas, later known as streetcar suburbs. Higher-ranking government clerks could now live in the country, enticed by healthy air, fine large houses, good schools and churches, and elegant private clubs.

Around the turn of the century, the *nouveau riche* built palaces and chateaus along the main streets and avenues north and northwest of the White House. These residences were mostly winter homes, places to reside and entertain during the season, that is, when Congress was in session. Fabulous parties were given for the politically powerful by the exceedingly wealthy.

Washington's new society had a social season that ran from New Year's Day to Ash Wednesday. Formal societies for literature, music, and the arts also were established, and there was a marked proliferation of social organizations and private clubs.

Washington was becoming an attractive place. Tourists came in droves. Students, scholars, and professors enjoyed the extraordinary intellectual resources including the libraries, universities, and scientific organizations. For professional men, the capital was a profitable place. Real estate speculators and land developers prospered. Inventors and scientists like Alexander Graham Bell, Herman Hollerith, and Walter Reed found Washington receptive and supportive of their ideas. Washington had ceased to be a village by the 1890s, and ". . . had risen . . . like a Uranian Venus."[4] By the turn of the century, the nation's capital was a proud place, described as a combination of old Babylon, new Philadelphia, and Versailles.

One man, more than any other in the history of the development of Washington, has been credited, blamed, and praised for transforming the city into a imposing national capital. "He lifted Washington out of the mud . . . he plucked [her] from the mire and set [her] as a jewel in the sight of men."[5] This man was " . . . the latter-day L'Enfant, with more brains and more power."[6] He was **Alexander Robey (Boss) Shepherd**.

Shepherd was six feet tall, powerfully built, and handsome. He had an indomitable will and ferocious energy. He was also known for his generous disposition, unrestrained laughter, engaging manner of speaking, and astonishing command of profanity.

A true love of Washington and thorough belief in the future of the capital city were driving forces behind Boss Shepherd. He was a Washingtonian, born in 1835 in the city's southwest section, called The Island. His father was a successful wood

and lumberman who died when Shepherd was only 10 years
old. The family was immediately reduced to poverty. Shepherd had to work a number of menial jobs to help support
his mother and siblings. At 17 years of age, he joined Washington's largest plumbing and gas fitting company, J.W.
Thompson. He proceeded to work his way to the top, then
bought the company. During the Civil War, he supplied the
government's needs and amassed a small fortune by the war's
end.

Shepherd invested in real estate and built over 1,000 dwellings between 1862 and 1872. He was the first man in Washington to build blocks of rowhouses throughout the city for
government clerks. He also purchased a country estate and
entered into politics. His power increased with his wealth.
One writer of the 1880s wrote:

> He [Shepherd] and his friends conceived the idea of mak-
> ing a great and beautiful city out of the slovenly and com-
> fortless southern town which the capital of the country then
> was. They first abolished the old municipal government . . .
> in its place they put a territorial government with a legisla-
> ture . . . [which] was merely a cover for the Board of Public
> Works, and of this board Shepherd was the head.[7]

Shepherd became the dominating figure on the Board of
Public Works. His own self-assurance gave people total confidence in him. With no training in engineering and a magnificent disdain for details, he wished only to implement his
comprehensive plan of improvements for the city ". . . as rap-
idly as possible . . . in order that in this respect the capital of
the nation might not remain a quarter of a century behind
the times."[8]

Construction work began in all sections of the city. Within
weeks, there were ". . . miles of incomplete sewers, half-
graded streets and half-paved sidewalks."[9] The extension of
the water mains, a new market house, and a new railroad
project were also inaugurated. In just six months, the new
government incurred an indebtedness three times that accu-
mulated by both Washington and Georgetown combined over
the last 70 years. Shepherd was indifferent to cost and he had

only one goal: to make Washington great. Besides, he believed in debts as a legitimate part of business.

In his haste, Shepherd incurred the wrath of a number of citizens. By 1872, properties were being overvalued and heavily taxed. Streets were being graded without regard to property owners' wishes. If the foundations of buildings were damaged in the process of grading, Shepherd ordered the owners to make them secure within 30 days, or have the building torn down at the owner's expense. Shacks and mansions suffered alike. When W.W. Corcoran's newly established *Louise Home* fell victim to street regrading, Corcoran got 1,000 signatures on a petition to Congress, which led to an investigation. The petition's results, however, amounted to no more than a slap on Shepherd's wrist.

The Washington Market Company was incorporated in 1872 by Shepherd in order to effect the building of a new market on Pennsylvania Avenue to replace the old Marsh Market. Known as Center Market, its rival was Liberty Market. Shepherd had the latter torn down one evening, and he invited all District Court Judges out to his suburban home so that no last-minute injunctions could be obtained. The new market he built was the largest and most modern in the United States.

Shepherd's real coup was removing the railroad tracks that crossed over Pennsylvania Avenue near the Capitol. They had been placed there temporarily during the Civil War. The railroad company, in defiance of Shepherd, placed an engine out on the crossing and left it there. One Sunday night, Shepherd ordered his workmen to tear up the track on both sides, leaving the engine stranded. Mr. Garrett, President of the B&O Railroad, was so impressed and amused by Shepherd's boldness that he asked him to be vice president of his company. Shepherd declined the offer.

An end came to Shepherd's steamroller administration in 1874. He had served as governor for only two years. President Grant appointed him to replace the first appointed governor, Henry D. Cooke, who stepped down after only one year in office. When national attention focused on Shepherd, another investigation was called for. The resulting 3,000 pages of fine print documented the proceedings. The city's territorial government was accused of being ". . . negligent, careless, improvident, unjust, oppressive, and illegal."[10] Heavy blame was laid on Shepherd for the financial disaster he had created. Congress set up a Board of Commissioners to govern the city. President Grant, loyal to Shepherd, then appointed him as one of the commissioners, but the Senate refused to approve it. As one Senator explained, "We would like to have confirmed Shepherd, but we felt that to give him any more money would be like pouring it into a sieve."[11]

Boss Shepherd had spent close to $20,000,000 in just three years, but in doing so, he forced Congress to participate in local expenses. The form of government established in 1878 by the Organic Act, set a fixed rate of federal contribution to the city for the first time.

After his stay in government, Boss Shepherd was broke. Worse than that, he was being taken away from his life's work of creating a real city out of mud. He sold most of his properties in Washington to settle his debts, and he moved to Chihuahua, Mexico, saying he would not return until he was rich enough to buy the whole city of Washington. In Chihuahua, Shepherd discovered a very rich silver and gold mine and more than recouped his fortune.

Although he lived the remaining 22 years of his life in Mexico, he did return several times to Washington. Shepherd left the city in such a state of disarray that Congress had no choice but to complete his work for him. During his time in office, 80 miles of roads had been paved, and 50,000 shade-trees had been planted. Pennsylvania Avenue was lined with elegant buildings where rows of wooden barracks-like structures once stood. Gardens blossomed and parks were filled with trees, fountains, and statues of heroes. New schools, churches, markets, and office buildings had been erected, and the sewer system was unequalled in the country.

Gas lights, which were installed by Shepherd, changed the way Washingtonians socialized, more than any of the other city improvements. Evening activities became popular from twilight dinner parties to late-night performances at the theater. Street improvements encouraged the construction of many magnificent mansions for the very wealthy. Washington held the title of the "Winter Newport of America" for 60 years, from the 1870s until the 1930s.

Boss Shepherd was given a grand welcome home in 1887 on his second return visit. Washingtonians staged a celebration unlike any before. There were fireworks and an evening parade with marching bands, working men in mud boots, the militia, and "200 men on bicycles rigged with wire frames on which hung lighted Chinese lanterns." People carried signs proclaiming "Washington suggested; Congress sanctioned; Shepherd made it."[12]

Boss Shepherd died in 1902 in Mexico, but his body was sent to Washington for burial in Rock Creek Cemetery. The citizens of Washington pledged funds to pay for a bronze statue of Shepherd to be placed in front of the new District Building. He was the first native Washingtonian to be so honored. The statue holds a map in one hand, and oddly enough, Boss Shepherd is perhaps the only politician to be represented in statue form holding the other hand behind his back.

In the last three decades of the 19th century, one man stood out among all the rest as leader of the Afro-American community in Washington and across the nation. At that time, black leaders were drawn to the capital city by Howard University as well as Federal patronage. "The talent and prestige of the Washington black community came to dwarf those in all other cities."[13] The most celebrated among those early black intellectuals who came and stayed was **Frederick Douglass**.

Frederick Augustus Washington Bailey was the elaborate name given to the baby born a slave in Talbot County, Maryland in 1818. His mother was a slave; his father, it was rumored, was the master of the plantation. As an infant, he was separated from his mother, who then walked 12 miles at night and 12 miles back before sunrise to visit her son. "These little glimpses of my mother obtained under such circumstances and against such odds," he wrote years later, "meager as they were, are indelibly stamped upon my memory . . . among slaves she was remarkably sedate and dignified. She was the only slave in Tuckahoe who could read."[14]

Frederick Douglass

In 1825, at the age of seven years, Douglass was sent to Baltimore to be a house servant. "I shall never forget the ecstasy with which I received . . . this information," he later wrote, "The ties that ordinarily bind children to their homes were all suspended in my case . . . my home was charmless; it was not home to me . . . my mother was dead . . . I left without a regret, and with the highest hopes of future happiness."[15]

In Baltimore, the mistress of the house taught Frederick Douglass the alphabet and the spelling of a few short words. Her husband was vehemently opposed to these lessons and Frederick Douglass later remembered the husband's words and his own reaction:

> 'If you give a nigger an inch, he will take an ell. A nigger should know nothing but to obey his master—to do as he is told to do. Learning would spoil the best nigger in the world. Now, if you teach that nigger (speaking of myself) how to read, there would be no keeping him. He would at once become unmanageable and of no value to his master. As to himself, it could do him no good, but a great deal of harm. It would make him discontented and unhappy.' These words sank deep into my heart . . . and called into existence an entirely new train of thought . . . from that moment, I understood the pathway from slavery to freedom.[16]

Frederick Douglass taught himself to read by befriending young white boys and converting them into teachers. When he was 17 years old, in 1835, he was sent to a different plantation and badly abused by the overseer. He explained his feelings concerning his first decision to run away from slavery:

> On the one hand, there stood slavery . . . feasting itself greedily upon our own flesh. On the other hand . . . under the flickering light of the north star, behind some craggy hill or snow-covered mountain stood a doubtful freedom—half-frozen . . . but when we permitted ourselves to survey the road, we were frequently appalled. Upon either side we saw grim death . . . now it was starvation causing us to eat our own flesh;—now we were contending with the waves,

and were drowned;—now we were overtaken, and torn to pieces by the fangs of the terrible bloodhound. We were stung by scorpions, chased by wild beasts, bitten by snakes . . . overtaken by our pursuers, and in our resistance, we were shot dead upon the spot . . . In coming to a fixed determination to run away, we did more than Patrick Henry, when he resolved upon liberty or death.[17]

Not until three years later in 1838 did Douglass succeed in escaping. Once in New York, he experienced ". . . the moment of highest excitement,"[18] only to be followed by the depths of loneliness. He adopted a motto, "Trust no man!" He felt totally alone, and wrote:

. . . without a home or friends—without money or credit — wanting shelter, and no one to give it—wanting bread, and no money to buy it,—and at the same time . . . pursued by merciless men-hunters, and in total darkness as to what to do, where to go, or where to stay—perfectly helpless both as to the means of defence and means of escape—in the midst of plenty, yet suffering the terrible gnawings of hunger,—in the midst of houses, yet having no home,—among fellow men, yet feeling as if in the midst of wild beasts, whose greediness to swallow up the trembling and half-famished fugitive is only equalled by that with which the monsters of the deep swallow up the helpless fish upon which they subsist.[19]

Help was given to Frederick Douglass ". . . by the humane hand of Mr. David Ruggles, whose vigilance, kindness, and perseverance, I shall never forget."[20] Douglass immediately wrote to Anna Murray, the free black woman with whom he had fallen in love in Baltimore. She came to New York and they were married. He was using the name of Frederick Johnson which he later changed to Frederick Douglass when he and Anna arrived in New Bedford, Massachusetts. There was plenty of work for him in the shipyards and elsewhere. With his first wages, he was able to subscribed to the newspaper, *The Liberator*. "The paper became my meat and my drink . . . [from it] I got a pretty correct idea of the principles, measures and spirit of the anti-slavery reform."[21] While attending an antislavery convention in Nantucket, Massachusetts, he was asked to speak to the group. "I felt myself a slave, and the idea of speaking to white people weighed me down. I spoke but a few moments, when I felt a degree of freedom, and said what I desired with considerable ease. From then until now I have been engaged in pleading the cause of my brethren."[22]

Douglass became a paid speaker, and in 1845, he published his autobiography, *Narrative*. In the book he mentioned by name his former master, who then came after him, claiming that Frederick Douglass was still his property. Douglass was forced to flee to England to avoid being captured as a fugitive slave. There he raised money to purchase his freedom, and within a few years, he returned to the United States as a free man. He moved to Rochester, New York, where he published *The North Star* newspaper. Douglass came to live in Washington in 1869 to become editor of another newspaper, the *New National Era*.

Washington was not an unfamiliar place to Frederick Douglass; he had visited the city many times before he decided to make it his home. On several occasions, Douglass had been given the opportunity to meet President Lincoln, and he even attended Abraham Lincoln's second inaugural reception, against the advice of some of his associates. It was a ". . . triumph of diplomacy . . . with Frederick Douglass blustering his way beyond politely obdurate guards into the presence of the president, who generously made the most of the occasion by humbly asking Douglass' opinion of the inaugural address."[23] He later wrote about Lincoln, "I was impressed with his entire freedom from popular prejudice against the colored race. He was the first great man that I talked with in the U.S. freely, who in no single instance reminded me of the difference between himself and myself."[24]

The Freedmen's Savings Bank in Washington needed someone to fill the position of president. In 1874, Frederick Douglass was offered the job. He respected what the bank symbolized and remembered his first impressions when he walked into the bank lobby: "The whole thing was beautiful . . . It was a sight I had never expected to see. I was amazed with the facility with which they [the colored clerks] counted the money; they threw off the thousands with the dexterity, if not accuracy of old and experienced clerks."[25] Unfortunately, even after he invested $10,000 of his personal fortune in the bank, it failed.

President Grant appointed Frederick Douglass to the Legislative Council of the new territorial government, which had been set up in 1871. This was the beginning of his public service and he found it necessary to put aside any thoughts of retirement. From 1877 until 1881 he was the U.S. Marshal of the District of Columbia, the first black man to hold that position. In 1881, he was appointed Recorder of Deeds of the District of Columbia; and from 1889 until 1891 he served the country as Minister to Haiti.

Opportunities were rarely missed by Frederick Douglass. He felt it his duty to speak out and write about topics that were important to him. The newspapers he published became an outlet for his convictions. His anger at some white people's imperceptiveness became the subject of one of his most earnest editorials in the 1880s. He called them "skin aristocrats" who displayed ". . . the inherent prejudices of slaveholders, [and who] violate the whole spirit of our institutions." He also blasted the professional colored community who snubbed those of their own race, saying ". . . the worst form of infidelity in regard to negro capacity is to be found among negroes themselves." He strongly believed in ". . . building a mutual understanding between the races"[26] through integrated education, and had to fight the black teachers who had a vested interest in keeping schools segregated.

Black initiative, Douglass felt, was being depleted through government welfare programs, and he spoke out against them. He wrote of problems arising from displays, like the Emancipation Day Parade, where, ". . . a vastly undue proportion of the most unfortunate, unimproved, and unprogressive class of the colored people . . . [are] thrust upon the public view . . . thereby inviting public disgust and contempt, and repelling the more thrifty and self-respecting among us."[27]

In his later years, Frederick Douglass was described as being ". . . one of the most striking-looking men in public life. He has coarse hair, as white as new washed snow, which stands out in a bush from his big head. He has an open and solemn face full of character. His black eyes look out from heavy overhanging eyebrows, and his mouth is firm and decisive. In speaking he uses good language, and his words are so chosen that they often bear quoting."[28]

After his wife Anna died, Douglass left Washington temporarily but returned to shock both black and white society. First, he moved to Cedar Hill in Anacostia into the former home of an avowed Negro hater, John Van Hook. Then he married Helen Pitts, a woman 20 years his junior, a former government clerk, and a white woman. Black society accused him of abandoning his race, but he and Helen were both extremely happy in their marriage despite the accusations.

Douglass continued to accept speaking engagements throughout his long life. On the day he died, he had already given one speech in the morning and was waiting for a carriage to take him to a second appointment that evening when he suffered a heart attack. The nation's capital was blessed to have had as a citizen, Frederick Douglass, "the most able statesman and most articulate man of his time,"[29] "the most influential man of his race,"[30] "the most sought after man in Washington."[31]

Many people made a name for themselves in post-Civil-War Washington. Government patronage and private enterprise offered great opportunities to those seeking to make something of their lives in the last third of the 19th century. One such entrepreneur was a young German immigrant, **Christian Heurich**.

The saint of beer in Brussels may be Gambrinus, but Christian Heurich was the saint of beer in Washington. He was born in 1842 in a 16th-century German castle that had been converted into an inn run by his father. He was orphaned when he was 14 years old, and with only a simple education in arithmetic and reading, he began a career in brewing that would continue the rest of his very long life.

Heurich apprenticed to a brewer and butcher for two years. With these skills, it was possible to obtain work and a good meal anywhere, so when he was 16 years old, Heurich began to travel across Europe on foot. He loved his freedom. He would stay in a city only as long as he pleased. When he found a place where he could learn something new about brewing techniques, he would stay for months or years. Beautiful Vienna on the Danube became his favorite among all the European cities in which he worked.

Heurich almost lost his life trying to come to America in 1866. After 10 years on his own, and with the encouragement of his sister, who lived in Baltimore with her husband, he booked passage on a ship from Liverpool. Just days after departure, a cholera epidemic broke out on the ship. More than 300 of the passengers died, and the ship returned to port. Heurich remembered similar epidemics in Vienna, where the brewmasters drank only beer and survived. So, Heurich drank only beer onboard the ship and returned alive, but rather inebriated, to England, crediting his escape from death to the powers of the brew.

Six weeks later, Heurich tried again to sail to America. This time he succeeded. He arrived sporting a handlebar mustache and goatee, which he wore for the rest of his life. He had little money, no job, and he spoke no English. He found work in a German brewery in Baltimore and invested his wages in savings, however, he found he was not learning English. "English was the language of the country," he wrote, "It was up to me to learn it properly."[32] He moved to his aunt's farm in Kansas to work and learn the language. A year later, he returned to Baltimore where he worked as a brewer, saving his earnings until he had $2,000 saved from his $35 monthly salary.

Heurich's character could be read in his stubbornness, his distrust for authority combined with a strong belief in himself, and his willingness to take risks. He modestly attributed his success to luck, but he wouldn't have been so lucky had he not worked so hard.

In 1872, Christian Heurich moved to Washington and rented a small brewery on 20th Street near M Street, Northwest. He hung out a sign and went to work. For months, sales were only about five barrels a day. Things turned around for him when the owner of the brewery, Mr. Schnell, died. Heurich bought the brewery and a little while later, he married Schnell's widow.

Heurich's work in the brewery never ceased. For 18 hours a day, seven days a week, he performed all the physical labor in the brewery. Because he was tricked by the German bankers who sold him the property, he had to pay double for it. He believed strongly in the quality of his product and therefore he unconditionally refused to advertise. He believed that only poor products needed advertising. He nearly went bankrupt waiting for people to discover his excellent lager.

Success and happiness did not always go hand in hand for Heurich. His marriage seemed more a marriage of convenience. He missed his homeland and longed to visit Germany again. Like most Washingtonians, he came from somewhere else and had little time to make friends. He made money, he invested in property, he built a bigger brewery, and he hired more workers. He encountered problems with the labor unions, for which he had no sympathy. He had made it on his own, and he expected nothing less from those who worked for him. His brewmaster once confronted him with a demand for more money. Heurich responded, "Listen here, Hans, if you were dead, what would I do?" "Hire yourself another brewmaster, of course," answered Hans. "But I don't see what that has to do with my demands." "Consider yourself dead," Heurich said.[33]

Sixteen years after arriving in America, Christian Heurich finally found the time and money to return on a visit to Germany in 1880. He was overworked, overwrought, and he had suffered a breakdown. There he was rejuvenated. Almost every year thereafter, he returned to Germany to the fresh air, good food, exercise, and spas. Altogether, he made 73 ocean crossings.

Heurich's wife died in 1884. On her gravestone he inscribed the phrase, *"Ach, sic haben, ein gute frau begraben, und dem gatten war sic mehr!"* (English translation: Oh, they have buried a good woman here, and for the husband she was more!) Three years later he married a young, beautiful woman. She was thrown from a carriage only a few months after they were married, and never fully recovered from the injuries she incurred. At the same time, his brewery suffered several fires, probably caused by labor disputes. The Young Women's Christian Association wanted his brewery out of the neighborhood.

Heurich's solution to these problems was to build the first fireproof building in the city, a brewery on the Potomac River near 25th Street, Northwest. His mansion near Dupont Circle, the second fireproof building in the city, contained fabulous rooms with wall murals and ceilings ornamented with cherubs, wood carvings, and marble mantles over never-used fireplaces, a curved onyx stairway, and provisions for an elevator to be installed for his old age. Soon after the mansion was completed, his second wife died.

In 1899, Christian Heurich married again for the third time. His third was the niece of his first wife, and the two had the same name, Amelia. She was 25 years younger than Heurich, and had grown up calling him "Uncle." After they were married, he had to remind her not to call him "Uncle" any longer. At 57 years of age, life began again for him. Heurich and his new wife were very much in love. They had three children whom he worshipped. They had a 15-room country house in Hyattsville, Maryland, where they passed the summers. He began to save newspaper articles written about people who lived to be 100 years old, wishing to live that long himself.

When the Prohibition Law was passed in the city in 1916, two years earlier than the rest of the country, Heurich closed his beautiful, castle-like brewery on the Potomac. He continued to produce ice in his large ice plant, however. Soon, with the advent of World War I, Americans of German descent became suspect, and Heurich was accused of being an enemy agent. He took refuge in his estate in Maryland. By then, he was 74 years old, and he had plenty of money, a dear wife, and adoring children. Washington forgot about him.

In 1933, prohibition was repealed. At 90 years of age Christian Heurich decided to start life anew. He reopened the brewery! He believed in good work and he believed in good beer. Washington welcomed him back. Values had changed, however; people became interested in his worth, not his health, and in the number of years he had lived, not how he had

Heurich Mansion

lived them. To those who would listen, he imparted this wisdom, "Practice moderation, even in moderation—and drink Heurich's beer."[34]

In 1940 Christian Heurich was honored in Washington for his 75-year business career. A whole section of Cissy Patterson's *Times-Herald Newspaper* was dedicated to the success of Heurich's brewery and its brewmaster. One advertiser wrote, "We toast Christian Heurich, Purveyor of Cheer, He holds the World's Record, For brewing Fine Beer."[35] Heurich lived to be 102 years of age and in 1945 he was the world's oldest active brewmaster. He worked every day, almost until he died. He never did have the elevator installed in his Dupont Circle mansion. Throughout his life, he often noted in his journals when describing himself, "You lucky guy! You lucky guy!"[36]

Although the old brewery was closed in 1956 and dynamited out of existence in 1961 to make way for the sleek new Kennedy Center for the Performing Arts, Heurich's lager has returned to Washington. Christian's grandson, Gary Heurich, is overseeing the brewing and distribution of this lager in the nation's capital. The legacy of the old "lucky guy" lives on.

Like Heurich, many businessmen came to Washington in search of their fortune. The **Lansburgh** brothers, who arrived in the 1850s were determined to show that hard work, integrity and customer service were the right ingredients for success. Lansburgh's Department Store lasted 110 years and became known as the oldest department store in Washington.

From Hamburg, Germany, the Lansburgh family emigrated to Baltimore. In 1854, while still living in Baltimore, 15-year-old Gus started working for Gutman's Dry Goods Store. The hours were long and the pay was poor and Gus decided he could do better. He opened a dry goods store next to Gutman's and advertised lower prices. A price war started between the two stores over hoop skirts. Each day, one or the other would mark down the price by a penny, until one day Gus put a sign in the window which read, "I will sell my hoop skirts two cents cheaper than the man next door."[37]

Washington lacked good merchants. Gus saw this need and moved to the capital city with his brother Max in 1857. Their

Lansburgh's Department Store

brother James soon followed. Gus carried shoestrings, buttons, bustles, and the like, selling them door to door from a backpack. The brothers rented a stall in Center Market on Pennsylvania Avenue. Soon they rented a tiny 10 × 15-foot space above the Bank of Washington building at 322 C Street, Northwest. In 1863 they named the store *Lansburgh & Brothers' Baltimore Bargain House.* An old photograph from those days shows most of the merchandise hung from nails on the walls. James replaced Max in the business, and he and Gus did everything: buying, marking, displaying, selling, and delivering.

On the evening of April 14, 1865, Gus and James heard that President Lincoln had been shot. They knew exactly what to do. They immediately left for Baltimore, which was a large textile market, and bought nearly all the black crepe and cotton fabric in the city. They returned to Washington the next morning. After President Lincoln died, the government requested that commercial establishments drape their storefronts with black bunting, just as the government planned to do on the federal buildings. Gus and James were ready to supply the city's needs. Even the engine and funeral cars on the train that carried Lincoln's body back to Springfield, Illinois, were draped in Lansburgh's black crepe.

The Lansburgh brothers rented a number of different storefront shops for their business, up and down 7th Street, Northwest. The name was changed to *Lansburgh & Brothers Metropolitan Dry Good Store.* Finally, they settled on just *Lansburgh & Brothers.* By the 1880s the brothers moved their store to a fine new location at 406-410 7th Street, Northwest, where they installed the city's first commercial elevator. At the grand opening, they promised to give a new silk dress to the first lady over the threshold of the new store. More than 1,000 people waited in line outside the entrance to ride the elevator and see who won the dress. When the doors were unlocked, the crowd surged forward with such force that the new plate glass display windows were shattered. "I remember the elevator," said Mr. Kahn, a longtime employee. "It was wooden and it was always getting stuck between floors. We had the first rotary door, too, but a woman caught her heel and said if we didn't take it out, she'd never shop there again. So we took it out."[38]

The two brothers worked very well together. James handled the financial matters and Gus handled the merchandise. Gus was known to disappear on buying sprees. He would tell no one where or when he was going, or what he was hoping to buy. Soon after, boxes, barrels, and bales would come pouring into the store; everyone knew then that Gus had returned from a successful trip.

Once he bought a *ton* of buttons, but thousands of them came off their cards. His brother James was very annoyed, thinking that the loose ones would have to be sorted through and sewn back onto the proper cards. Gus had a different idea. He hired a carpenter to build a huge bin. Then he had the remaining buttons stripped from their cards. He dumped all the mixed-up buttons into the bin and offered them for sale at five cents a quart. It was a bonanza! The ladies of Washington flooded the store for a chance to pick through the buttons in the bin.

Gus became a nationally known silk buyer. Lansburgh's carried the largest stock of silk in the city. As the store expanded, the brothers built a one-story structure with a hugh skylight so ladies could see the silk in natural light. Gus' son, Mark Lansburgh, or Mr. Mark, as he was called, remembered, "That skylight was fine when the sun was shining, but when it rained, the wind would blow the rain in through the vents. Then we'd have to run around covering all the tables and putting out buckets."[39]

The Lansburgh brothers had a motto: "A customer's money does not belong to us unless the customer is entirely satisfied."[40] They also had the first return policy in Washington. There were a few customers who tried to take advantage of this. Gus' son-in law, Mr. Ralph Goldsmith, reminisced, "We sold a customer one of those Charlie McCarthy dolls. She brought it back, three days later and said she'd had it all that time and it hadn't said a word."[41]

Mr. Mark related a story of one problem he had with the return policy:

I worked as a floor man in the millinery department. In those days, the hats had heavy silk linings under velvet. They'd have birds of paradise or egret or ostrich feathers, and they were so big they had to be held on with hat pins. A woman would bring one of these hats back and say her husband didn't like it. I'd look at the lining, and there would be a dozen holes from the hat pins. The question was whether to point out the pin holes or take back the hat.[42]

He also explained how he was taught to handle dissatisfied customers: "They told me in the service department if a woman was sitting down she wouldn't be half as mad. One time, a customer was angry and I was pulling over a chair so she would sit down. She took the chair and threw it at me. I ducked and it skidded right across the waxed parquet floor into a show case."[43]

The Lansburgh family members were strong believers in fair treatment for their employees. In 1867, when the store was just seven years old, they placed their first newspaper advertisement announcing that the store would ". . . close on weekdays at six and one half p.m. for the convenience of the clerks."[44] In the summer, they often gave the employees Saturdays off. They instituted the 10-50 Year Club to pay tribute to faithful employees.

Lansburgh's *By Jupiter* program gave monetary incentives to workers for the extra kindnesses they showed to customers. Herman Neugass (Gus' daughter's son-in-law) remembered a story about a *By Jupiter* award recipient. The young salesman was sent out to help a customer and ". . . when he got there, the woman complained of feeling feverish. She said she felt so bad she hadn't fixed herself a thing to eat for a day and a half. He got a thermometer and took her temperature. She was running 103 so he called the doctor. After that, he went in the kitchen and fixed her some broth and tea. She wrote us a letter about it."[45]

The *By Jupiter* program was the reason behind the harp music heard in the store several times throughout the day. One salesman explained that all employees were told the story ". . . about a man who was grouchy all day and the Greek gods ask him if he'd like to live the day over. Well, he

does, and every time he's about to lose his temper, there's
Jupiter strumming his harp. Then he remembers to be courteous, and he has a much better day. So when we hear the
harp, we're supposed to remember."[46]

Lansburgh's customers were a loyal group. At the turn of
the century, Gus and James began holding anniversary parties at the store. They celebrated by giving away glassware
with Lansburgh's name on it. Barrels of glassware would be
shipped from Philadelphia: pickle dishes, egg cups, toothpick
holders, and other specialty items. Long lines of people came
to the store to get a free piece of the glassware. Half a century
later, a salesgirl recalled, "During World War II, we had to
figure out some way to ration nylons. We decided to sell them
to our customers on an alphabetical basis. Women would
come in and say they should get some nylons because they
were old customers. To prove it, they showed us those old
pieces of glassware."[47]

The Lansburgh family was a large and popular one in
Washington. Gus' father, S.M. Lansburgh, was chosen rabbi
of the Washington Hebrew Congregation. Gus had 13 children, many of whom became involved in the business, as did
the sons-in-law. One son, Julius, formed his own furniture
business at the turn of the century. In 1921, he moved his
store at the corner of 9th and F Streets, Northwest, in the old
Masonic Temple building. His customers included kings,
presidents, princes, and diplomats.

Another of Gus' sons, Sol Lansburgh, or Mr. Sol, became
president of the company and worked there until past his 85th
birthday. Mr. Sol's brother, Mr. Mark, served as secretary and
occasionally as architect of renovations using his degree in
architecture from the University of Pennsylvania. Both
Charles Goldsmith and his wife, Aunt Minnie, who was Gus'
daughter, played an active role in the business, as did their
son, Mr. Ralph. Four other grandsons and several great-
grandsons also worked there later.

Perhaps none of the Lansburghs was better remembered
by Washingtonians than Henry Lansburgh, or Call-Me-
Henry. Around the store, there were so many Mr. Lansburghs, that policy had always been to call them by their first

names with a Mr. in front of it. Call-Me-Henry was the only one to go against policy. In fact, he encouraged people to use this sobriquet by handing out little cards with Call-Me-Henry on it, entitling the bearer of the card to a five-pound box of candy at Brownley's Confectionary on F Street, Northwest. His brother, Mr. Mark said, "I've seen letters simply addressed 'Call-Me-Henry' without even 'Washington, DC' on them and they'd be delivered. He used to give away American flags with inches of real gold for fringe. When World War I ended and soldiers turned up in Washington without any money, they were always being sent to 'Call-Me-Henry.' "[48] He was also known to give soldiers money for a meal, or even enough for a ticket home if they needed it.

At one time, Henry was a buyer of women's clothing. If he heard a crash in the store, he would rush right over. If a someone had dropped a package of china and glassware and it had broken, Call-Me-Henry would slip some money to a salesgirl and tell her to replace it. This was true even if the glass had come from the dime store. When Call-Me-Henry died in 1925, he was buried in Rock Creek Cemetery. His headstone is marked only with the name, Call-Me-Henry.

During the 75th anniversary celebration for Lansburgh's, a great luncheon was held at the Willard's Hotel with 300 people in attendance. Mr. David Owens, president of the National Retail Dry Goods Association, made this remark: "Lansburgh's has always pioneered in taking the modern things of the modern day and enable them to serve better their employees and their customers."[49] Gus and James, who died in the early part of the 20th century, would have been very pleased with that assessment.

The Willard family's hotel was the site of many special celebrations as well as the temporary residence for many of Washington's distinguished visitors. **Henry Augustus Willard** was a born host, and together with his brothers, became Washington's most famous hoteliers. Although Henry was a pioneer in the field of hotel management, he came into the business in an unusual way.

Remarkably innovative and with a keen sense for detail, Henry was ready to seize any opportunity to better himself.

While serving as a steward on the Hudson steamship *Niagara*, he discovered a better way to serve his guests. He provided them with reading materials to help them pass the time. In this way, Henry created the first floating lending library. For each book borrowed, he charged a small fee, and by the end of his third season on the ship, he had made $2,000. Another modest business for Henry evolved out of a need by people in Troy, New York, and New York City to have packages, messages, or valuables carried between the two Hudson River ports. For a small fee, he guaranteed safe transport of the item, and so established the first overnight delivery service.

Miss Phoebe Warren of Troy met Henry Willard on a Hudson River cruise and was quite impressed with him. She introduced him to her fiancé, Benjamin Tayloe of Washington, D.C. Tayloe owned a hotel near the White House built by his father, John, as an investment in 1817. The location was excellent, but there had been five managers in 30 years, and none could seem to make the hotel a success. Tayloe offered management of the hotel to Henry Willard.

Henry accepted the challenge and moved to Washington in October 1847. He brought his brother Edwin with him, and within a few months, another brother Joseph. Then yet a fourth brother, Caleb arrived. They all worked hard to develop a good reputation, and in a few years they purchased Tayloe's property. The name was changed from Fuller's City Hotel to Willard's City Hotel; soon it was known just as Willard's.

Henry maintained the philosophy that if you want to hold your patrons, feed them! The meals were lavish at Willard's as recalled by Henry's son:

> Hotel-keeping was very different in those days from what it is now; almost every morning at three o'clock, my father would be called to go down to Center Market to buy provisions and supplies for the hotel; then at meal hours, especially at dinner, he did the carving, and in this way no waste occurred. Everyone was interested and worked.[50]

By 1852, Henry began to search for top government men to stay at his hotel. ''If only I can get General [Franklin] Pierce at my house, I shall be all right . . . in a few days we shall know if Pierce is the President."[51] Pierce was one of many presidents who eventually stayed at the Willard's. Presidents Taylor, Fillmore, Buchanan, Lincoln, Taft, Theodore Roosevelt, Wilson, Coolidge, and Harding all stayed at the hotel. Many Vice Presidents also made Willard's their home.

Next door to the Willard Hotel was a Presbyterian church. When the church was put up for sale in the 1850s, the Willards bought it. They converted it into Willard Hall for concerts, theatrical productions, and political meetings. Jenny Lind, the Swedish nightingale performed there and stayed at the hotel. She was so popular that President Fillmore stopped by to see her, and Daniel Webster asked her out.

The first Japanese delegation ever sent abroad arrived in Washington in 1860. The Willards were asked to make all the arrangements for them, so the hotel assumed the role of the national guest house. Sixty rooms were refurbished and redecorated, a special entrance was set aside only for their use, security was placed around the hotel, and kitchens and dining rooms were prepared for the visitors; the Japanese, however, brought their own cooks. After they left, the Willards received complaints from their staff that the rooms had to be thoroughly cleaned and repapered because of the excessive amounts of hair oils the Japanese used on their hair.

One of the greatest parties ever held in Washington was given in 1859 at Willard's for the departing British ambassador and his wife, Lord and Lady Napier. More than 1,800 people paid $10 each to attend this event. It was the last social occasion on which high-ranking government officials of the North and South met under friendly circumstances. Northern and Southern congressmen both lived at the Willard's, but one floor and one exit were used exclusively by the Southerners, and another floor and exit by the Northerners. Henry, however, always flew only the American flag over the hotel.

Throughout the month of February 1861, Willard Hall was used by delegates to the Peace Convention. What remained of the 36th Congress met there under the chairmanship of ex-President John Tyler. Their hope was to reach an agreement

on a workable plan for peace and bring the Union back together to avert war.

Abraham Lincoln arrived in Washington the night before
his inaugural and he stayed at the Willard's. Rumors of as-
sassination plots against the new president led Lincoln's security men to take every precaution. His suite at the Willard's
later became officially known as the Presidential Suite. When
Henry Willard visited Lincoln in the suite that night, he asked
if there was anything Lincoln needed. Lincoln requested a
pair of slippers, but since the president's feet were so large,
a regular pair would not do. Henry rushed to see his wife's
grandfather, William C. Bradley, who had the biggest feet in
town, and borrowed a pair of his slippers for Lincoln. The
next day, the slippers were returned with a note of thanks;
they are still in the Willard family.

Willard's was the busiest place in the city during the Civil
War. Generals, congressmen, statesmen, newspapermen,
poets, novelists, and inventors stayed there. Nathaniel Haw-
thorne wrote that ". . . the Willard's Hotel could more justly
be called the center of Washington and the nation than either
the Capitol, or the White House, or the State Department."[52]

Julia Ward Howe came to Willard's Hotel with her husband,
Dr. Samuel Gridley Howe. While they were visiting
McClellan's Army Headquarters in Virginia, the infantry
marched by singing a haunting song, whose first line repeats
three times: "John Brown's body lies a'mouldering in the
grave . . . But his soul goes marching on." It was suggested
to Julia, a well-known poet, that she write more appropriate
words for that song. She returned to the hotel, and awoke
early the next morning, sat down at the writing desk, and
composed the words to the *Battle Hymn of the Republic*, which
she sold to the *Atlantic Monthly* for $10. Willard's was the first
hotel in America to provide its guests with desks.

Julia's brother, Sam Ward, was also staying at the Willard's
during the war. He was ". . . acquainted with everybody of
importance in Washington, and on intimate terms with many
of the most influential men of the day, he exercised the art of
persuasion through his engaging personality . . ."[53] His skill
in conciliation was so well known that it is said Abraham

Lincoln sent him with the British diplomat William Howard Russell to tour the South early in 1861 with the hope of avoiding war. This mission proved unproductive. While staying at the Willard's, Sam Ward was often seen in the lobby with very wealthy clients who sought him out for favors. He became known as "King of the Lobby," and could be considered Washington's first lobbyist. General Ulysses Grant is credited with naming men like Sam Ward lobbyists.

The Willard brothers became personally involved in the Civil War effort. Edwin lost his life while serving in the Union Army in 1863. Joe became a major and was stationed in Fairfax. There he met and fell in love with Antonia Ford, the young daughter of a local merchant. Unknown to him, she was considered one of the best Confederate lady spies. Jeb Stuart made her a member of his staff with a signed letter, dated October 7, 1861:

> To Whom It May Concern:
> Know ye: that reposing special confidence in the patriotism, fidelity and ability of Miss Antonia Ford, I, James E.B. Stuart . . . do hereby appoint and commission her my honorary aide-de-camp, to rank as such from this date . . . She will be obeyed, respected and admired by all the lovers of a noble nature.[54]

John S. Mosby received intelligence from Antonia including the location of cavalry regiments. Because of her work, Mosby was able to pull a surprise attack on General Edward Stoughton, as he and his officers slept in the town of Fairfax. Mosby took them prisoners of war.

Secretary of War Edwin Stanton was infuriated by Mosby's action. He sent Lafayette Baker to round up spies. A newspaper article written by one of Stoughton's men named Antonia Ford as a spy. She was foiled by a female spy sent by Baker, and Stuart's letter was used as evidence against her. For seven months she was held in the Capital Prison. Major Joseph Willard finally arranged for her release through his friends. The two lovers had a pact. She would take the oath of allegiance to the United States, and Joe would resign from the Army. They were married soon thereafter.

Joe and Antonia had one son, Joseph, and two daughters. Unfortunately, Antonia never quite recovered from the time she spent in prison, and she died in 1871. Joe was devastated. He became reclusive. He sent the children to be raised by Antonia's family in Fairfax. He worked harder than ever with the hotel, conducting all of the dealings with the banks. He invested wisely in real estate and amassed quite a fortune. The brothers were among the richest men in Washington. By the 1880s, Joe, who was known to hoard his money, was said to be worth between $7 and $10 million. Henry was worth $1.5 million, and Caleb, just $1 million.

Caleb left his two brothers in the 1850s to buy William E. Ebbitt's boarding house just across 14th Street. He kept the name, Ebbitt House, and it was often used as an overflow hotel for Willard's. Joe later bought out Henry and continued to run Willard's efficiently. Henry then opened the Occidental Hotel, just next door to Willard's. Henry's son, Henry K., eventually took over the business, and his two sons, Henry A. Willard, II, and William, came in to manage their father's estate.

Joe's daughter, Belle, married Theodore Roosevelt's son, Kermit in 1913. They often stayed at the hotel. Kermit's habit was to bring a book of poetry to the breakfast table. A waitress asked him about it one day, and he replied, "Poetry does for the mind what a bath does for the body. It freshens and cleanses. Read it each morning before you start out and you'll begin the day better." Joe's other daughter, Elizabeth, married the son of the fifth Earl of Caernarvon, the Egyptologist who discovered the tomb of King Tut-ankh-amen.

Joe's son became a lawyer in Fairfax County, Virginia, and inherited a fantastic estate when Joe died in 1897. The old hotel was not fit for the 20th century, however, so the famous New York architect, Henry Janeway Hardenberg, was asked to design a new, grand hotel. In 1900, construction began. The hotel became Washington's first commercial skyscraper, with the city's largest ballroom occupying the top floor.

"The three most important things to see in Washington are the Capitol, the White House and Willard's Hotel,"[56] stated an old guidebook. The Willard brothers are gone, but their

The Willard Hotel

name lives on in Washington. Although Willard's was closed for more than a decade, in 1981 it was bought and renovated at tremendous cost. Today, The Willard Hotel is again worthy of the titles given it years ago: "the Crown Jewel of the Avenue," "the marble poem in the sky," and "the gathering place for the great, the near-great, and those who aspire to greatness!"[57]

Chapter 4

Culture, Money, Depression, and War

T he first half of the 20th century was an explosive time in Washington, socially, economically, and especially culturally. Between 1910 and 1935, many new museums and concert halls were dedicated, including the new Smithsonian Institution building, now called the Natural History Museum, the Freer Gallery of Oriental Art, the Folger Shakespeare Library and Theater, and the Coolidge Auditorium at the Library of Congress. During the same time, the Daughters of the American Revolution built Constitution Hall which is Washington's largest concert and lecture hall, with a seating capacity of 4,001.

Washington's population increased dramatically before 1950. New public parks and picnic areas were created throughout the city. The popular summer spots included the fashionable Meridian Hill Park, Griffith Baseball Stadium, and the bathing beach near the Tidal Basin. By the 1920s, the Belasco Theater, the new National Theater, and the Howard Theater all added tremendously to the entertainment scene.

The beautification of Washington became a serious concern in the early part of the 20th century. Japanese cherry blossom trees were planted around the Tidal Basin. They were a gift to Washington from the people of Japan in 1912. The National Capital Park and Planning Commission was created in 1920, and the Fine Arts Commission was organized a few years earlier. The Lincoln Memorial was under construction from 1915 until 1922.

Washingtonians became more socially conscious. Many influential local citizens tried to educate their fellow Washingtonians on important social issues, such as the deplorable alley dwellings that existed in nearly every neighborhood. Many charitable organizations, which were established around the turn of the century, became very active by the 1920s. These included The American Red Cross, The Board of Charities, and the Junior League.

In 1912, the sinking of the *Titanic* brought a symbolic end to an era. Woodrow Wilson became president, and with his administration came revolutionary changes. The Victorian years were over and there was a strong desire for a forward-looking perspective. During this period, power became centralized in Washington, and the city came to have a voice in world affairs. Gone were the once-dominant insular feelings, as Washington matured into a world-recognized national capital city.

America's entry into World War I changed Washington forever. With the arrival of the government "girls," there was a great need for housing and more office space. Temporary buildings were constructed between the Washington Monument and the Lincoln Memorial site. They were used for 50 years, creating quite an eye sore on the otherwise attractive landscape. There was a new mobilization of wealth, manpower, and industry, which resulted in the establishment of new government agencies.

Prohibition touched Washington between 1916 and 1933, but not seriously. Congress was only mildly affected by it. Private parties were rarely affected, and embassies were completely untouched.

After World War I, there was a desire to return to normalcy. Government building projects flourished. The Federal Triangle construction program of government buildings on the south side of Pennsylvania Avenue employed a great number of people throughout the 1920s and 1930s. West of the White House in the Foggy Bottom neighborhood, the Department of Interior, the Federal Reserve Building, and the National Academy of Sciences all received beautiful new marble and granite office buildings. Rowhouses and apartment buildings shot up to meet the needs of the multitude of new government workers.

With the arrival of the Great Depression, social life, as established in the city during the 19th century, essentially ceased to exist by the mid-1930s. Many of the magnificent mansions along Massachusetts Avenue were put up for sale. The only buyers seemed to be foreign governments that needed new quarters for their embassies. Many of these old palatial homes were converted into both offices and residences for the ambassadors. Still, Washington had quite a few very wealthy residents who continued to live unaffected by the changes around them.

Washington's population has always radically increased because of wars or economic depressions. Two world wars and the Great Depression rocketed the city into a new dimension. It emerged as a powerful and cosmopolitan metropolis during the 1940s.

World War II transformed the nation's capital into the command center of the United States. For the first time since the Civil War, the city was fortified. The population exploded to 950,000 residents. More temporary buildings were added to the old ones near the memorials. Large, uninhabited homes were commandeered by the government and used for war offices. The new Pentagon building was suddenly alive with offices, shops, and restaurants to serve the 40,000 workers stationed there. Barracks-like apartment complexes were hastily erected in the nearby suburbs. Large homes or apartments were broken down into rooming houses.

Washington in the 1940s had become a lively and exciting world center. The new airport on the Potomac became a popular place; the main attraction was the huge new restaurant. The opening of the National Gallery of Art in 1941 exposed a whole population to the beauties of western European masterpieces. In 1944, the Dumbarton Oaks Conference, which occurred at the Dumbarton Oaks estate in Georgetown, set the stage for the establishment of the United Nations. Significant changes were visible in the new diplomatic corps sent to the capital city. When the war ended, Washington began to relax a little, and feelings of restrained optimism were combined with a sense of confidence in the future of the nation.

There have always been men and women of talent and wealth who came to live in Washington, but not many can claim to have made their fortunes there. Between 1899 and the beginning of the Depression, **Harry Wardman** amassed a fortune of more than $30 million. "Why, I have found out there is so much money lying around loose in Washington that I can pick it up off the streets," he said.[1]

He told a reporter of the *Philadelphia Public Ledger* in 1921, that he had been born in Bradford, Yorkshire, England, but

> I ran away from home when I was seventeen. I worked in my father's dry goods store; I was raised in the dry goods and textile industry. Perhaps I got too much of it, though I've been able to make use of the experience I got. Anyway, I left without a word to anybody. I was going to Australia; I was going to work my way as a cabin boy or something. But when I got to London I learned there wouldn't be a boat from England for a month. So I decided then and there on America. I spent almost all my money getting to Liverpool. When I got there I found the old steamship *Britannic* was just pulling out for New York. I walked right on her and stayed on and when I got to New York I got off. Nobody noticed me and I wasn't registered anywhere. I walked right on that old boat and rode free across the ocean and walked right off again, right on into New York. I had seven shillings, or $1.75 as capital to go on. So I got a job in a department store.[2]

From New York, Wardman travelled to Philadelphia. The building profession captured his interest, and he apprenticed as a carpenter. Stairbuilding became his specialty, and he soon became a supervisor of other workers. The 1893 Colum-

Wardman Towers

bian World Exposition attracted Harry to Chicago, and by 1895, he moved to Washington. In 1897, he was listed in the city directory as a carpenter living in the Brookland section of Northeast Washington. Local architects hired Wardman and kept him busy building staircases in houses they designed. Among them was the flamboyant T.F. Schneider, who, in 1889, built the Cairo Hotel, the first and tallest steel-framed private building in Washington. Schneider recognized Wardman's talents and encouraged him to go out on his own.

About this time, a tailor, Henry Burglin, wanted a new house built. Wardman convinced him that he could build it for less than anyone else. The job was done well. Burglin recommended Wardman for other jobs and helped him obtain financing through the Home Savings Bank run by B.F. Saul. Herbert T. Shannon and Morton Luchs became early associates of Harry Wardman. Together they began a real estate business. With the help of sales of so many Wardman houses, their firm became the largest in Washington. Harry Wardman did confess that ". . . while getting started from less than nothing, I worked 20 hours out of 24."[3]

With a fellow Englishman, Wardman was able to build a row of several houses on Longfellow Street, Northwest, just at the turn of the century. Harry and his partner each made nearly $5,000 profit, a large amount in those days. Wardman had his first taste of success. His partner returned to England, but Wardman went on to build more and more rows of houses, and then he began developing whole neighborhoods. When asked in 1925 if he knew just how many houses he had built, his answered vaguely, ". . . between forty-five hundred and five thousand." Eventually, he was credited with having built 9,000 dwellings.

Harry Wardman happened to have been in the right place at the right time, and he possessed the right skills to take advantage of the situation in the early 1900s. Washington had a real shortage of good, affordable houses after World War I. Wardman recognized the city's need and acted upon it. Becoming a little over-zealous, he started to encroach upon parkland early in 1924; the city became nervous. Apparently he tried to work with the local commissioners; but when Congress failed to purchase some land set aside for possible park use, Wardman announced he was moving ahead with his development plans. The land in dispute bordered Rock Creek Park near the National Zoo. His threatened development forced Congress to act. In June 1924, Congress created the National Capital Park Commission, with the authority to acquire parkland.

Always alert to new building opportunities, Wardman was one of the first to realize the need for apartment houses. He built 400 of them. Some say this was his most important contribution to the city. In 1925 a story in *The New York Times* explained,

> Twenty years ago, Washington was a city of boarding houses. A play of that time graphically set out Washington life. It was called, 'The Little Gray Lady' and told the story of a Government clerk and a boarding house. Harry Wardman conceived the idea that Government workers would rather have modest homes than live in boarding houses. He would build plain apartment houses for them. There should be apartments as small as one room and bath. The one lone Little Gray Lady who wanted her own home should have it, and a gas stove on which to poach her breakfast eggs.[4]

Wardman installed mechanical refrigerators as standard equipment in his apartments, which, for the first time, were rented to families with children. He built apartments for middle-income tenants, but he also built many apartments for the wealthy. The Northumberland in Northwest was one of the first luxury apartment buildings he constructed. Opened in 1909, the Northumberland was the first apartment house to have showers in every apartment. The Dresden was another of Wardman's apartment buildings. Its decorative plaster work was so expensive that he never tried it again. In 1913, he built the Avondale, one of the first luxury apartment houses, which he traded to Mrs. E.J. Walter for a number of downtown properties. He had invested $175,000 in building the Avondale, and in exchange, received properties valued at $275,000. Wardman built an empire by making deals like this.

Wardman's Cathedral Mansions was considered the largest apartment house complex south of New York City. The property extended nearly one-quarter of a mile along Connecticut

Avenue, Northwest. Finished in 1923, it contained nearly 500 apartments.

Eight years earlier, Wardman conceived a grandiose scheme. He planned the largest apartment complex in the United States, the Wardman Gardens. The complex was to have been a series of five high-rise towers built on 20 acres of land near Connecticut Avenue and Calvert Street, Northwest. Altogether, there were to have been 10 buildings, each seven stories high, encircling a large courtyard. It was a $5 million project that included 1,250 apartments, parks, tennis courts, playgrounds, a ballroom, library, gymnasium, and public dining room. Unable to obtain financing for the complex, Wardman instead, began construction on the site for the Wardman Park Hotel in 1917. It was modeled after the Homestead Hotel in Hot Springs, Virginia. The Wardman Park became Washington's largest apartment-hotel, and the fifth largest in the United States, with 1,100 rooms, nearly 600 baths, and a 300-car garage. A roof garden, Turkish bath, billiard room, drugstore and grocery, tearoom to seat 100, and dining room to seat 500 were also part of the hotel. The lobby was 200 feet long and 45 feet wide. Ninety percent of the rooms were designed to receive sunlight during the day.

The Wardman Park Hotel played host to many early television programs. *Meet the Press*, the *Today* show, the *Camel News Caravan*, and the *Arthur Murray Dance Program*, all got their start there. Scenes from the movie *Advise and Consent* were also filmed there.

Wardman's own house was located on the property where he built the hotel. It was a magnificent mansion designed by Albert Beers in 1909. Spanish in style, the house had a green tile roof and a long cascade of stairs with plantings at every landing. Seventeen years later, while his wife and daughter were in Paris, Wardman decided to raze the house to make way for Wardman Towers, another luxury apartment building. The architect, Mirhan Mesrobian, designed the fantastic complex in the 18th-century Georgian domestic style, complete with Palladian windows and rich limestone trim. It was called the home for the rich and famous. Many high-ranking government officials resided at Wardman Towers, including

Henry Cabot Lodge, Clare Boothe Luce, Lyndon Johnson, Hugo Black, John Foster Dulles, Dwight D. Eisenhower, Barry M. Goldwater, Dean Rusk, Robert A. Taft, Earl Warren, Herbert Hoover, and Adlai Stevenson.

Wardman became diversified by the 1920s. He oversaw the Harry Wardman Real Estate, Rentals, and General Insurance Company; the Wardman Construction Company; the Wardman Real Estate Investment Corporation; the Wardman Mortgage and Discount Corporation; and even Wardman Motors, Inc., which sold and serviced the Willys-Knight and Overland motor cars in 1926. Wardman explained his business organization in a 1921 interview:

> Our business here, which is now being extended to Detroit and Buffalo, is organized like a department store. There are departments, each with a responsible head. We have our own architectural department, our own finishing mill . . . [and there are] the excavators, cementers, painters, and the other groups, all of which are kept busy throughout the year, under individual heads, who report to me.[5]

Older buildings in need of repair became challenges to Wardman. He described himself as a "junk dealer" and explained, "I buy old buildings, rags of buildings, bones and bottles of discarded houses, and turn them into habitable, homelike dwellings and apartments."[6]

Harry Wardman financed his operations during the 1920s with borrowed money. In an advertisement run in *The Evening Star* for the sale of stock in the Wardman Mortgage and Discount Corporation, the stock was called, "Safe—Sure—Successful. We are not speculating—not even taking chances on good or bad judgement in investing these funds. The reputation of the Wardman Construction Company is such that anyone will agree its programme provides ample assurance . . ."[7]

Wardman began to have financial problems in 1929 when several Wall Street firms sued him for a commission in connection with the flotation of the Wardman securities. His empire began to crumble. He was forced to give a large hotel operator his choice properties to manage. During the next year, he lost almost everything. An article in *The Evening Star* quoted him as saying he was ". . . through with the apartment and hotel business."[8] Then it listed some of the properties he lost, including the Wardman Park Hotel, the Carlton Hotel, the Hotel Roosevelt, the Chastelton Hotel, the Hotel Annapolis, and apartment houses containing more than 7,000 rooms.

Two years later, in 1931, he was called to testify before a Congressional subcommittee investigating his mortgage refinancing amid charges of fraud concerning $13 million worth of securities. Wardman responded, "I am a carpenter, a builder, and engineer, a contractor. [Financial] books bore me . . . All I know is we pay big income taxes. That means we make big money . . . I did the building work and signed the papers when they were put before me. All that [financial] stuff was foreign to me." He blamed his financial mess on the "gangsters, gunmen and three shell men" who had taken over his business. "I thought I was a rich man," he said, "and then I woke up and found I didn't have a nickel."[9]

Wardman was known as a generous man. Several minor diplomats were allowed to reside at the Wardman Park for years, paying little or no rent. He tipped the employees with $50 bills. After he lost his fortune, he did not give up. Rather, he went back to work building more houses. His reputation in the business community was still sound. During the Depression, he built 900 small houses, many in the Fort Stevens area off Georgia Avenue, Northwest. He was on his way back to financial recovery when he died of cancer in 1938.

Wardman was called a great builder and a visionary who built magnificent buildings. "Harry Wardman built some of the landmarks of the city of Washington,"[10] commented Henry Brylawski, former chairman of the District of Columbia's Landmarks Committee. His list of accomplishments include 4,000 free-standing, semidetached, and row houses; 400 apartment buildings, 12 office buildings, 8 hotels (including the Hay Adams and the Jefferson), 2 clubs (including the Racquet Club, now the University Club), 2 important hospital annexes, 2 embassies (including the Embassy of Great Britain, of which he was exceptionally proud), and 1 large parking garage. He named all of these buildings himself. He was also responsible for tearing down a number of beautiful old buildings and houses, like the two fine H.H. Richardson Romanesque Revival homes of Henry Adams and John Hay on Lafayette Square.

"Much of the present physical appearance of Washington is due to this remarkable, self-made man, whose style and accomplishments have never been equalled in Washington architecture,"[11] wrote James Goode, historian and former curator of the Smithsonian Institution. When Wardman died, one out of eight city residents lived in a building constructed by Harry Wardman. "He was the colossus of Washington real estate," noted *The Washington Post*. He was "far and away the outstanding builder in the history of Washington," commented *The Washington Herald*, and an obituary in *The Evening Star* contended, he "probably did more than any other man to promote the residential development of the capital."

About the same time Harry Wardman was energetically building up the city of Washington, another great man was quietly building an extraordinary collection of art for Washingtonians—and the world. **Duncan Phillips** brought modern art, or in his words, art that is "forever modern," to the nation's capital.

The second son of a Pittsburgh industrialist, Duncan Phillips came to Washington as a child in 1896. His father, Major Duncan Clinch Phillips, had been ill, and he was advised to find a milder climate. The winter of 1896 in the nation's capital was a relatively warm one, and the major decided to make Washington his home.

The Duncan Phillips' family was comfortably wealthy. Phillips' maternal grandfather was James Laughlin, a banker and one of the founders of the Jones and Laughlin Steel Company. Phillips' father was a manufacturer of window glass. Huge plate glass window were incorporated into Major Phillips' Washington home, designed by architects Hornblower and Marshall. The sunlight coming through the windows transformed the interior into a sunny and cheerful sanctuary.

The Washington in which Duncan and his brother, Jim, grew up was a tranquil, sleepy place. The two boys were very

The Phillips Collection

close. In fact, Jim waited two years before going to college until Duncan was ready, so they could go together. They attended Yale, graduating in 1908. Duncan studied English literature, but he was also interested in art history. His dream was to be an essayist on the subject. He felt strongly that art was a neglected topic at Yale, and he was overwhelmed by the "deplorable ignorance and indifference" to art among the students. He recalled one student announcing ". . . that Botticelli is a wine, a good deal like Chianti, only lighter . . . He was rudely awakened by a sensitive friend to the fact that Botticelli is not a wine but a cheese."[12] While in college, he wrote many essays on the subject of art. Just after he graduated, he wrote one more letter to the class secretary in 1908,

> I have lived in my home in Washington . . . devoting much study to the technique of painting and history of art . . . At Madrid, London, and Paris as well as New York and other cities. I have met and talked with many artists in their studios and gone the round of exhibitions. [In my writing] I have attempted to act as interpreter and navigator between the public and the pictures, and to emphasize the function of the arts as means for enhancing and enriching living.[13]

In 1910, Duncan and Jim decided to visit the Orient with the aim of collecting Japanese prints. By 1912, they had traveled extensively, and had seen Cezanne's and Matisse's work in Paris. Duncan found their art too radical, however, and wrote that he much preferred the "genuinely progressive" American paintings. He immersed himself in books on the subject of art, and wrote serious essays on the spirit of Impressionism and the revolution in modern painting.

The brothers were given a yearly allowance of $10,000 with which to purchase paintings. Their father advised them to look for "good art with something to say." Phillips found a painting by Arthur B. Davies entitled, *Visions of Glory*, which he purchased, and then wrote an essay on the artist. He met with Davies, and in a speech to the American Federation of Art in 1917, he skeptically reported,

> Davies recently took my education in hand and gave me an elementary object lesson. He brought out a framed pic-

ture of a young girl playing a violin—one of the exquisite
things of his early period. On the glass he marked in chalk
the contour of the masses and then removed the glass. The
diagram was not unlike an artist's masterpiece. And Mr.
Davies said in all seriousness that the skeleton of form contained all the aesthetic emotion suggested by the subject but
now the rhythm was released from all extraneous interest
[and] from all sentimental irrelevance.[14]

Suddenly the world of Duncan Phillips was thrown upside
down. In 1817, on the same day his brother was married, their
adored father died. Less than one year later, in 1918, Jim died
of influenza. Duncan was in shock. "What pulled him back
was the thought of creating a memorial," said his wife. Later,
Duncan wrote,

There came a time when sorrow almost overwhelmed me.
Then I turned to my love of painting for the will to live. Art
offers two great gifts of emotion—the emotion of recognition and the emotion of escape. Both emotions take us out
of the boundaries of self . . . At my period of crisis I was
prompted to create something which would express my
awareness of life's returning joys . . . I would create a collection of pictures—laying every block in its place with a
vision of the whole exactly as the artist builds his monument
or decoration . . . a joy-giving, life-enhancing influence, as-
sisting people to see beautifully as true artists see.[15]

Duncan Phillips hurled himself into the new responsibility
of collecting art works to share with the world. The Phillips
Memorial Gallery opened to the public late in the fall of 1921
with 240 paintings. Two large rooms in the house had been
set aside specifically for the display of the collection. The
atmosphere was homey. There were couches and plush chairs
to sit on and tables with ashtrays. Phillips wanted everyone
to feel at home, to be comfortable in this little gallery. The
rest of the house was lived in by his mother, his wife, Marjorie, who had studied art in New York, and himself.

The museum was unlike any other museum in the United
States. For the first time, the works of living artists were
featured. On display were paintings by Chardin, Monet, and

Sisley, together with Weir, Ryder, Davies, Whistler, and Hassam. According to Phillips' son, Laughlin,

> The paintings originally purchased, and all those to follow were chosen not necessarily because they were widely acclaimed, historically significant or radically innovative, but because they impressed my father as beautiful products of a particular artist's unique vision. His increasingly catholic taste excluded the academic and faddist, but honored 'the lonely artist in quest of beauty, the artist backed by no political influence or professional organization.'[16]

Over the next 10 years, more than 600 paintings—nearly 40 a year—were carefully collected by Phillips and his wife, Marjorie. Actually many more than that number were acquired over the years, but they were later traded back to the artists or dealers. Phillips traded for other examples of the artist's work that he felt were, in some way, better. The collection has been rightly called "one of the world's greatest one-person museums." All decisions about the collection, purchases, and exhibitions were made by Phillips, although his wife was always consulted. "I have no advisors, and I have no agents at all among the dealers. The capacity to decide for oneself is one's only safeguard against the contagions of fashion in art . . . My special function is to find the independent artist and to stand sponsor for him against the herd mind."[17]

It was during this time of revolution in art during the 1920s that Phillips made many major purchases. In 1923 he bought *Luncheon of the Boating Party* by Renoir, *Uprising* by Daumier in 1924, and *Mont Ste-Victoire* in 1925 by Cezanne. He was encouraging to all the struggling young painters and local artists who came to him. He often bought their paintings and placed them in his "encouragement" collection. "Having no trustees to consult," Duncan wrote, "I need not worry about making mistakes . . . It has been my policy and I recommend it to my successors, to purchase spontaneously, and thus to make mistakes, but to correct them as time goes on. All new pictures in the Collection are on trial, and must prove their powers of endurance."[18]

The unusual method Phillips created for hanging paintings caused his visitors to think and enjoy each work as it interacted with others. He moved them around from room to room, so they could be seen at different times in different kinds of light. He did not want one painting to be associated with any particular room. Phillips often installed his paintings in "units." Klee's works were displayed together as a unit, as were the Bonnards. Sometimes he put artists of the same periods together, or artists whose color schemes were similar. He always wanted an interaction among the paintings; they seemed to carry on conversations with each other. Phillips was careful with each selection. He explained,

> One of my methods is to have sent on approval quite a number of canvases by a painter who interests me . . . and then to hold several long and silent sessions of observation and reflection while waiting for each to speak . . . It helps decisions to shift paintings around from room to room, from one light to another, to see them all together and to test how socially adaptable they are.[19]

There were times when the words of artist Robert Henri haunted Phillips: "The vision and expression of one day will not do for the next. Today must not be a souvenir of yesterday. And so, the struggle is everlasting." Phillips responded, "Often I wonder what I will think of my decisions of today ten years from now. I can only live and think and act according to the degree of sound judgement and aesthetic sensitiveness given to me from day to day."[20]

Eventually the collection grew so large that Phillips had to make a decision on where he was going to house this very personal collection. He chose to let his collection take over the whole house; he, Marjorie, and their son would move out and find a new home in 1930. "Again and again I have stressed the unassuming simplicity and domestic comfort of the place," Phillips wrote. He established his sanctuary museum, as a "haven for those who enjoy getting out of themselves into the land of artists' dreams."[21]

One block from the Phillips Collection was the home of **Alice Roosevelt Longworth**. No other woman in the 20th century made a more powerful impression on Washington than Alice. She expressed her opinions freely and delighted in

Alice Roosevelt Longworth's Home

unconventionality. She was in the media spotlight for nearly 80 years. The reporters adored her, from the day she arrived in the city, as daughter of the Vice President, until her death in 1980. They gave her the title of Princess Alice. Her escapades often overshadowed her father's political accomplishments, a fact that did not please Theodore Roosevelt at all. Her own family considered her ". . . a hellion . . . capable of doing almost anything to anyone at any time."[22]

Alice was Teddy Roosevelt's first-born daughter. When her beautiful mother, Alice Lee, died from complications of childbirth; her father gave the newborn baby to his sister to raise. Theodore Roosevelt remarried in 1887, when Alice was three years old. Her father seemed not the least bit anxious to bring the child back into his new life, and she was not enthusiastic about returning. For whatever reason, however, his new wife, Edith, was determined to raise the child. Edith was pregnant five times, always somber and ill during Alice's childhood, which was not a happy one. Alice described herself as, "a shy, uncomfortable child." Although she never lost her shyness, Alice did develop a flamboyant outer layer.

The most popular song of the day, during her father's administration, was named for her, "Alice, Where Art Thou?" Her favorite color, a grey-blue, was copied for evening gowns and called "Alice Blue." She thoroughly enjoyed becoming a regular subject for the worst gossip sheets across the country, perhaps because it irked her stepmother, who believed one's name should be in the paper only three times: to announce one's birth, marriage, and death.

The young friends she made in Washington were romantic and exotic. Maggie Cassini was the daughter of the Count de Cassini, the czar's first ambassador to the United States. Alice liked her all the more when she became the subject of a Washington scandal. It was rumored that her mother was the count's housekeeper. Maggie described their friendship as having the ". . . violence of a bomb . . . a combination of two heedless girls who used their position thoughtlessly to impose their fads, their caprices on everyone—a veritable reign of terror."[23]

Cissy Patterson was another friend, the daughter of a Chicago newspaper millionaire. Alice, Maggie, and Cissy were frequently invited to parties together and became known as the Three Graces. All were spectacular flirts. Congressmen often "courted all of them at the same time." The inventor, George Westinghouse, threw a party for the three in New York. He asked them to write the guest list which they made so long, that Westinghouse, in order to accommodate the party, felt obligated to add an annex to his huge ballroom.

Alice's manners were deplorable. On one occasion, she interrupted her father three times in his office while he was in conference with author Owen Wister. When asked why he was unable to look after Alice more, he replied, "I can be President of the United States—or—I can attend to Alice."

Roosevelt was known to admonish his daughter often with his "fearful lectures," as she called them. During the summer of 1904, Alice was visiting wealthy friends in Newport, Rhode Island, while President Roosevelt was trying to crusade against the "malefactors of great wealth." Alice's escapades with the sons and daughters of the very wealthy, who were Roosevelt's target, made the papers. Her father sent Alice such an angry letter that it "scorched the paper on which it was written . . . [as he] . . . enumerated the iniquities that I had committed."[24]

Secretary of War William Howard Taft asked Alice to accompany his party on a trip to the Far East in 1905, which was officially called an inspection tour of the Philippines. She knew Nicholas Longworth would be along. She was 21 years old, and felt it was time to get married. He seemed the most likely candidate.

In 1906, Nick and Alice were married in the White House. "I wasn't excited, I wasn't nervous. It was another big party and I had been to big parties," she said. She slept until noon, although the wedding was at one o'clock. She described the East Room as looking like a funeral parlor, and her emotions, she said, fluctuated between "animation and grimness." The only real show of the day was when Alice grabbed the sword from Major Charles McCawley's sheath and flamboyantly sliced through the wedding cake.

The happiness of marriage ended when the honeymoon ended. Nicholas Longworth was a popular man among his peers and among the ladies of Washington. As Speaker of the

House of Representatives, he earned the respect of both political parties, together with the attention of many women. He was 15 years older than Alice, and had always considered himself a lady's man, even after he was married. Nick's infidelities became well known.

Alice was terribly hurt by Nick, but she stubbornly declared, "I was never terribly in love . . . I was interested in politics, so I thought marrying a politician would be much better than marrying someone else."[25]

Nick was an excellent violinist, but Alice described a musical evening with him as "boring to the point of stupefication." Her favorite instrument was the banjo and her favorite song was her father's theme song from his rough-riding days: "A Hot Time in the Old Town Tonight." Serious music for her was a Strauss waltz or a Sousa march. Alice did, however, like to dance! At one White House party in 1911, a Congressman's wife reported Alice wearing flesh-colored stockings and an electric blue satin gown. She reported that Alice " . . . held the very scant skirt quite high, and when the band played, kicked about and moved her body sinuously like a shining leopard cat." At Mrs. Leiter's ball, she did the turkey trot with a cigarette hanging from her lips. As she bounced across the dance floor, she blew little puffs of smoke into the air. Someone said "Alice looked like a steam engine coming down a crimped track."[26]

"All of Nick's friends were sort of middle-aged drunkards . . . they thought it manly or something," noted Alice. "I saw a great deal of drunkenness, and it disgusted and angered me"[27] Before she was married, Alice drank quite a bit, but later she watched as her Uncle Kermit, cousins Stewart and Monroe, and brothers Ted and Kermit all became alcoholics.

For fun, Alice founded a group called the "Night Riders" in 1910. She and ". . . her pals, all on horseback, had taken to galloping into the front yards of friends and acquaintances [late at night] . . . Howls and cat calls continue until the house is opened and the refreshments are served." It became the highest social honor to be paid a visit by Alice's "Night Riders."[28]

An affair between Senator William E. Borah and Alice was no secret. At age 41, gossips branded her as Aurora Borah

Alice. She became pregnant for the first time, and was quoted as saying that she would try anything once. Few people even considered that the child could be Nick's, especially when she suggested naming her De-borah. The child, Paulina, was born on Valentine's Day 1925. Alice, never pretending to like babies, conferred the responsibility of raising the child on a nannie.

Oddly enough, Nick and Paulina adored each other. He took her to his office at the House of Representatives nearly every Saturday. When Nick died suddenly of pneumonia, the ten-year-old girl was devastated; her mother seemed relieved. After Nick was buried in Cincinnati ("Sin-Sin-Nasty," as Alice called it), she immediately burned all his papers and his most precious possession, his Stradivarius.

Within a week of Nick's death, Alice was asked to run for his seat in the House. She refused. She made the excuse that she did not want to join the ranks of widows who were ". . . using their husbands' coffins as a springboard into the House or Senate . . . [and] I was never good at remembering names and that's fatal in politicians." A newspaper reporter wrote, "Alice would make . . . a rotten candidate because she doesn't like people and won't shake hands. Can you imagine Alice Longworth going around kissing babies?"[29]

Alice had a difficult time showing affection to her daughter. Just as her father had destroyed all memory of her own mother, Alice destroyed all memory of Nick for Paulina. The little girl became fearfully shy. A childhood acquaintance of Paulina's once said, "I can't imagine anybody I'd sooner not have as my mother than Mrs. L. As a mother she was lethal. She was immensely selfish . . . [and] had bullying qualities."[30]

Paulina married Alex Sturm in 1944, when she was 19 years old. Alex began to drink heavily and Paulina began to drink with him. Their daughter, Joanna, was born in 1946, but that did not deter their drinking habits. In 1951, Alex died of cirrhosis of the liver. Six months later, Paulina tried to commit suicide but survived. She joined the Catholic Church and threw herself into volunteer work to help the impoverished, but she suffered another nervous breakdown a few years later. One evening in 1957, Joanna returned home to find her mother had died; some people said she committed suicide.

Alice insisted the death was an accident and blamed herself for Paulina's failings, but was overjoyed at the prospects of raising Joanna. For Alice, who was nearly 73 years old, it was a second chance at life. Joanna was terrified of her grandmother. Alice would do handstands, imitate animal noises, hop over sofas, and play all sorts of games in order to win Joanna's attention.

Over the years, Alice and Joanna became nearly inseparable friends.

Alice never gave up her interest in politics. She called Eisenhower a "nice boob," and told Richard Nixon to grab the vice presidency. Nixon, who was often a guest at Alice's home, observed that politics discussed at Alice's dinner parties "more in terms of the excitement of the battle—who was going to win, etc., than in terms of which side ought to win." Someone noted that Alice "aligned herself with anybody who was on the way up and cut herself off from anybody on the way down."[31]

Katharine Graham, publisher of *The Washington Post*, is quoted as saying, "The Kennedys met her, and were enchanted by her. She was very spoiled by them. She got asked to dinner and put on Jack's right. They treated her with great respect, admiration and affection." Bobby Kennedy declared Alice to be "my favorite person in Washington."[32] From Bobby, that was an amazing statement, since Alice teased him mercilessly, knowing how much he disliked it.

Alice became a fan of Lyndon Johnson's. She said, "He's a masterful man, the greatest I've ever seen at getting things done, and I've seen them all." Alice had no party loyalty. When she announced that she voted for Johnson in 1964, she wondered out loud if the DAR would revoke her voting privileges. President Johnson had a tendency to kiss the ladies. Alice's broad-brimmed hat had frustrated his attempts, and he complained to her, "I can't kiss you under that hat." She briskly answered, "That's why I wear it."[33]

Until just a few years before her death, at the age of 96, invitations to Alice's teas were highly prized. On her 90th birthday she said, "I'm a hedonist. I have an appetite for being entertained." To these little parties, Alice invited people who were good conversationalists. She was always on the lookout for a good story or scandal. Someone once gave her a pillow on which had been embroidered the phrase, "If you don't have anything nice to say, please come sit by me."[34]

Alice Roosevelt Longworth and **Eleanor Medill (Cissy) Patterson** were friends in Washington during Theodore Roosevelt's administration, though in their latter years they exchanged many barbs. Alice once said, "Cissy's life was so much richer than mine. I said a lot of things, but Cissy *did* them."

Cissy had determination coupled with a sense of adventure, an abundant imagination, and more than enough money to carry out her ambitions. Cissy's mother was a wealthy, strong-willed, socially ambitious beauty from an important Chicago family, the Medills, owners of *The Chicago Tribune*. Her father was just the opposite in character; mild-mannered, philosophical, and thoughtful, he had worked his way up in the newspaper business and married the boss' daughter. He could handle almost anything in life except his wife, who eventually drove him to drink and a nervous breakdown. She was a powerful influence on her two children, Cissy and Joseph.

Cissy was tall, straight-shouldered, and immaculately groomed with beautiful red hair, which she piled on top of her head. "Watch the way that girl moves," Theodore Roosevelt once whispered to his daughter Alice, "She moves as no one has ever moved before." Someone noted that, "Cissy always walked as if the air parted in front of her!"[35]

Cissy's upbringing was very strict, but when she was 17 years old, she escaped her mother's control. She traveling to Europe to visit her aunt and her uncle, who was the ambassador to Austria. At a party there, Cissy met Count Josef Gizycki. He was ". . . handsome, well-built, very literate, fluent and widely read in many languages . . . but most of all he was sexual. I think it was the main interest in his life. He was amoral and cynical, but he was a marvelous lover," said a countess who knew him well. She warned Cissy that he was reputed to be ". . . one of the most dangerous men in the empire."[36] But the stories, intended to frighten her, fascinated her instead.

Her Aunt Kate tried to warn her, "This country is rotten with titles. In England, a title amounts to something; only the eldest child gets it. But here every child has the same title as its parents. Besides, these Continentals make wretched husbands—the worst in the world."[37] Despite all the warnings, Cissy and the count became involved, and they announced that they planned to marry.

The Pattersons were strongly against the marriage. Gizycki came to America to force the issue, and after months of preparation, the couple was married in her parents' Washington home. The count was in his glory. After the ceremony, Gizycki returned to his hotel. Hours passed; he did not come back to the party. Then he telephoned, demanding that his wife meet him at the railroad station. It seemed that there had been a misunderstanding about the dowry he was to receive. The money, nearly a million dollars by one account, had not been deposited. He was leaving for Russia without her.

The dowry agreed upon, Cissy and Gizycki left together for Russia, where Gizycki's castle turned out to be just a plain, big, old, white building. Cissy was miserable. Gizycki proved to be a drunkard, a rogue, and a wife-beater. Cissy took solace in horseback riding and reading novels. Although the count was well-read, and he scorned reading novels, saying, "Why should I? My own life is all the novels of the world rolled into one." When Cissy accused him of having a mistress, he replied, "I shall go to see any girl I like, anytime I choose to. You have no money, you have no children, you have no sense. You are no good as a wife. You bore me to death."[38]

After more than a year of marriage, Cissy became pregnant. The pregnancy was difficult; she was ill all the time and alone, even at the birth of her daughter, whom she named Leonora Felicia. Cissy's mothering instincts were not strong, and the child was cared for by servants. In 1907, after two years of marriage, Cissy decided to change her life. She took the baby to London, but Gizycki had her followed and took the child back. The newspaper headlines proclaimed, "Count Kidnaps Baby."

Gizycki filed for separation in 1908, but getting a formal divorce was nearly impossible in Russia at the time. Besides, he wanted the child. The scandal made Cissy a celebrity in Europe and America. Cissy's mother wrote a pleading letter to President Taft who had been a Yale classmate of her husband. She requested his intervention in the return of her granddaughter. Taft immediately sent a handwritten letter to Czar Nicholas. The czar responded by bending the law to order the count to give up the child to her mother. When Gizycki refused, he was put in jail. Forty-eight hours behind bars was enough for him; he agreed to surrender the child.

Felicia and Cissy then moved back to Chicago, but by 1915, Chicago had become too quiet for Cissy. Her friend, Alice Roosevelt Longworth, urged her to come back to Washington. Cissy and Felicia moved into her mother's 40-room mansion on Dupont Circle. The following winter she had to face the grueling details of the divorce trial. After her divorce was final in 1917, she carried on a brief affair with William Borah, the same senator with whom her friend Alice Longworth was involved.

Cissy's mother moved from Washington back to Chicago, and left Cissy the great home on the circle. Cissy began writing articles for *Harper's* and *The Atlantic Monthly*. She also wrote quite a successful novel, *Glass Houses*, about Washington society.

Felicia married journalist Drew Pearson in California, with Cissy's blessing. They moved back to Washington where their daughter was born, and where Drew worked as a reporter. About the same time, Cissy decided to marry a close friend, lawyer Elmer Schlesinger. One morning in April of 1925, Cissy called Felicia and Drew. "We're getting married this morning. Come on over." Felicia didn't believe her, but Drew stopped by, and was the only witness to the event. Cissy reported, "I'm happier than I ever was before." In less than four years, however, Elmer died of a heart attack. Not long thereafter, Felicia and Drew were divorced.

Cissy liked Drew, and he became her favorite escort following his divorce from her daughter. Drew was 34 years old and Cissy was 50, but she acted like his contemporary. Drew later married Luvie Moore Abell and gained custody of his daughter, whom Cissy adored.

Cissy continued to enjoy the creativity of writing and published another novel, *Fall Flight*, in 1928. The story was based on her youth and first marriage. One reviewer wrote, "When a second novel shows such a marked improvement over a first . . . and when the first was in itself a first book of unusual skill and brilliance, the author may be said to be established as an American novelist of note."[39]

In another endeavor, Cissy made up her mind that she wanted to buy *The Washington Herald* from William Randolph Hearst. Hearst's response was that he liked to buy newspapers, not sell them. She persevered and went to visit Hearst at his estate, San Simeon, in California. She did not succeed in convincing him to sell, but she made a good friend. During the stock market crash of 1929, Cissy's investments were barely hurt as her money had been invested very conservatively; Hearst, however, was badly damaged. She appealed again to Hearst; this time he offered her co-editorship. She said she must be editor, not co-editor. Hearst agreed.

"Out to sea in a tub," is how Cissy described herself as editor, but she went to work with full force. "There is nothing in the contents of a newspaper that a woman cannot understand. No part of the paper to which she cannot contribute, no part of a newspaper management that need necessarily be beyond her power to control,"[40] she stated in an interview. She often said that she would rather raise hell than vegetables, and she often electrified the newsroom by her very presence. She printed a front-page editorial entitled, "Interesting But Not True," filled with barbed remarks about Alice Roosevelt Longworth. It was the first of many such editorials. Washington was aghast, Hearst was delighted, and Alice found it "very amusing."

Drew Pearson had become a successful syndicated columnist by this time. Cissy featured his column on the editorial page. The column, named for his book, *Washington Merry-Go-Round*, was printed in 600 newspapers with a combined circulation of 40 million subscribers. Subsequently, Cissy and Drew began to argue over issues involving World War II. One of Pearson's editorials was cynically critical of Douglas MacArthur whom Cissy admired. She sent the order to the copyroom, "Pull it out. The hell with it. If I have to print opinions opposed to my own to stay in business, I'll get out." Drew protested and asked her to cancel his contract with the paper. Cissy agreed. Cissy later called Drew Pearson, "one of the weirdest specimens of humanity since Nemo, the Turtle Boy . . . for years now we have had to keep our gila monster away from him because in a battle of fangs, it wouldn't be a fair fight." Then she added, that he was "America's outstanding journalistic heel."[41]

She used *The Herald* to focus on issues no one else would report on: venereal disease (her reporters interviewed prostitutes and doctors' clinics), cleaning up the Potomac, getting home rule for Washington, eliminating the slums, the civil rights struggle, and dealing with police corruption.

In one year's time, Cissy had made *The Washington Herald* one of the most provocative newspapers in the country. She went on to start a travel page, a column on beauty hints, and a men's fashion page. She promoted a column called, "The Male Animal," to give advice to brokenhearted men in which she published the first letter in an American paper on homosexual problems. She encouraged independence among reporters, letting them come up with their own assignments. When one of her staff complained or showed interest in something, she would say, "Write a story about it!"

The Herald became Washington's most popular newspaper under Cissy's guidance. In 1939, Hearst agreed to let her buy it, and along with *The Times*, which she had controlled for several years. *The Herald* was a morning paper, and *The Times* was an evening paper. She merged the two papers into one, saying to her readership, "I hope you will like the new *Times-Herald*, Washington's only around-the-clock newspaper."[42] Actually, it was the first in any large city.

For nine more years, Cissy continued to run the newspaper. When she died in 1948, this little poem was published in the *New York Daily*:

She was gay and she was witty,
She was wise and she was pretty,
Now she's dead, let's not flout her,
Let's not say dull things about her.[43]

The obituaries called her "the greatest editor in America" and "the most powerful woman in the country." One reporter explained, "She enjoyed power. She misused it frequently, but I will say, in the way she misused it, you could get mad, but somehow you enjoyed it, whether you were the brunt of it or not. There was a liveliness to it . . . Cissy was a publisher who dared to be daring." She was called both a street fighter and a grande dame.

The nation's capital was known to be a hard-drinking city from its earliest years. Washington's first pub, Rhodes Tavern, was opened near the White House only months after the arrival of Congress. From 1917 until 1933, local, and later national, laws against the sale of liquor were enacted, but seldom enforced. Prohibition seemed to inhibit no one's drinking habits in the city, least of all the senators and representatives. One man in particular is remembered for keeping Congress happy during those dry years. He was called the Man in the Green Hat. He was **George L. Cassiday**.

For more than a century, temperance groups had lobbied to make the city an example for the nation. There were parades and displays. A Temperance Hall was built in 1843, and Dr. Henry Cogswell privately paid for the establishment of a Temperance Fountain in 1880, which was to have flowed with pure, cold drinking water, but proper plumbing was never installed. On November 1, 1917, the Sheppard Act became a law in Washington, prohibiting the sale of liquor within the city limits. The act was passed two years before the Eighteenth Amendment, which prohibited drinking throughout the nation.

Washington's "Rum Row" was hard hit. This saloon area was located near F Street, Northwest, near the Treasury Building and across the street from most of the local and national newspaper offices. The Ebbitt House Bar, Shoomaker's Saloon, Roche's Wine Bar, Dennis Maloney's, the Lawrence Hotel's beer garden, and Frau Gerstenberg's Half-Dollar Dinner Restaurant were all forced to close, together with 290 other drinking establishments and liquor stores. Within just a few months, however, the number of illegal drinking places doubled the number of those that were closed. Twenty years later, there were ten times as many.

Since Washington had a two-year head start over the rest of the nation in dealing with the situation, Washingtonians became expert on brewing and distilling alcoholic beverages. The nation's capital had became a huge "home laboratory," commented a newspaper columnist, where common conversations often centered around the exchange of distiller's secrets, how to spot a speakeasy, or how to connect with a reliable bootlegger. A speakeasy guide to the city was published by *Collier's*.

Cissy Patterson's *Washington Herald* newspaper reported that

> Cocktails continued to be served as usual. In fact, it became a point of honor to serve cocktails. Folks seemed to imagine that if they didn't serve cocktails other folks would think they were obeying the law, and such a thought, to a liberty-loving people, was naturally unbearable. So people served cocktails under prohibition who had never dreamed of serving them in their own homes before. The grand fiasco of the prohibition experiment was already becoming apparent.[44]

During Prohibition, there was definite peer pressure to visit the fashionable clubs. Social status often was judged by one's embassy connection or knowing the right bootlegger. *The Charlotte News* reported that, "Washington is wet. I mean it is wringing, dripping wet. Intoxicants are sold in cafes, drugstores, hotels, and almost everywhere." Congress was the wettest place in town. George Cassiday, a young man whose mother was a member of the Women's Christian Temperance Union, or the WCTU, became the most notorious, most colorful, and most well-connected bootlegger in the business.

Cassiday came to Washington after World War I, hoping to return to a job he held before the war. He was described as a handsome, outgoing man. In his search for work, he met two Congressmen who asked if he could help them buy some liquor. Virginia and Maryland's whiskey was easily obtainable. Soon he was serving a number of Congressmen, and started going to New York and Philadelphia regularly to purchase good quality spirits.

Cassiday became a trusted, respected, and revered man about town. Congressmen kept him so busy, that a member of the House of Representatives suggested he take an office in the House Office Building. He was given keys to congressmen's offices so that he could make deliveries discretely, and had more congressional keys than anyone else who worked in the building. As many as 25 deliveries a day kept him busy. In the House, he also operated an elite club called the Bar Flies Association that met every afternoon for card playing and drinking. Membership was selective, just as it was to Speaker of the House Nicholas Longworth's club called The Library or The Board of Education, which promoted bipartisan unity through drinking.

Cassiday was in demand at all times of the day and night. He spent more time in the House Office Building than did most of the congressmen. He took representatives' constituents on tours of the Capitol, supplying them with liquor (for individuals as well as for convention parties), and even pouring them a drink or two in a congressional office. "Some of them got a real thrill out of having a drink under the shadow of the Capitol dome. It was something they could tell about when they got home,"[45] said Cassiday.

Problems did occur for Cassiday. Someone broke into his House office and stole $600 worth of liquor. Occasionally bottles would break in transport, since he hand carried most of his supplies from New York or Philadelphia on the train. His first arrest caused him a bit of a setback. In 1925, three mem-

bers of Congress became a self-proclaimed antivice committee. They apprehended Cassiday while he was delivering liquor to another congressman. At the time of his arrest, he was
wearing a green felt hat. The House sergeant of arms mentioned to a group of reporters that a man in a green hat had
been taken into custody for bootlegging. Cassiday served a
brief time in prison, and when released, Nicholas Longworth
banned him from the House of Representatives Office Building. He moved on to the Senate, where for another five years,
he continued his trade out of an office in the Senate Office
Building.

In February 1930, Cassiday was arrested again. *The Washington Herald's* headline read, "Bootlegger Stalked by Butts for
Weeks." Roger Butts was a 20-year-old prohibition agent
whom the press dubbed the Dry Spy. He had been placed in
the Senate for the sole purpose of driving Cassiday out of
business. Prohibition Commissioner James M. Doran and
Hoover's Vice President, Charles Curtis, gave the order to set
up an espionage system to cut off the source of senatorial
liquor. Butts went to work in the Senate stationary room as a
clerk because rumor had it that Cassiday stored his liquor
there. After a few days, he was introduced to Cassiday. Once
he tried to buy a bottle of gin for $3, but the money was
returned in place of the gin. Cassiday was suspicious.

Later, Butts met another bootlegger, Mr. Goldberg, who
readily sold him a bottle of wine. When Butts reported this
to his superior, he was told to concentrate on the Man in the
Green Hat. "Everybody was sure that the Man in the Green
Hat was the principal source of supply for the Senate," said
Butts. One of Butts' coworkers agreed to cooperate in catch-
ing Cassiday. "The next morning, February 18, my friend
called Cassiday and told him to deliver six fifth bottles of gin.
He told him to put it in his car which was parked in the back
of the building at 11 o'clock,"[46] recalled Butts. When Cassiday
made his delivery, he was met by "Lone Wolf" Asher, a well-
known, zealous federal prohibition agent. The Man in the
Green Hat was seized, together with his little black book.

Cassiday's black book became a great source of fascination
and speculation in Washington and across the nation. It was

said to list all of Cassiday's customers, their preferences, and favorite delivery points. Iowa Senator Smith Brookhart launched a campaign to have the book's contents published, thus making the Man in the Green Hat a national figure. He was paid to write his memoirs for *The New York Evening World*, which published them in installments and became the most popular story of the day. Months after the arrest, *The Washington Herald* ran the headline, "Green Hat Man Buyers' List Vanishes." The article reads,

> The gentlemen on Capitol Hill who have been worrying that the list taken from George Cassiday, 'The Man in the Green Hat,' and said to revel the embarrassing fact that many prominent in the nation had been purchasing illicit liquors from him, may rest easy. For it was learned today, that 'list' just ain't . . . it was never in the possession of the government . . . Roger Butts never saw the fateful list . . . It was the arrest that gave rise to the rumor that his list had been seized . . . [when] Cassiday was taken to the police precinct house and booked, as is the custom, his property was taken away from him and locked in the station safe. And among his belongings taken were a small note book which may or may not have contained startling information . . . But Cassiday secured bond and as is the custom, his property was returned to him when he was freed.[47]

Roger Butts published his side of the story in *The Washington Herald*. He stated that ". . . he entered on his mission with the spirit of a true crusader." When asked what inspired him to become the Dry Spy of the Senate, and he responded, "When I was 15 I went to a sorority party given at the Wardman Park Saddle Club. I certainly got an eyeful of what liquor could do . . . I saw young people getting drunk and acting silly . . . It sort of turned me against liquor . . . I was afraid of making myself foolish." Butts continued, "Most people nowadays feel sort of harshly toward prohibition agents," but, he said he had learned a lot from the experience, and philosophized, "I found that politics play a big part in the enforcement of the prohibition law. It sort of made me feel that the law could never be enforced as long as politics were allowed to enter into the thing."[48]

The retirement of the Man in the Green Hat was not the end of drinking on the Hill. John Nance (Cactus Jack) Garner, who later became Franklin Roosevelt's Vice President, used to invite the newspaper reporters to his office to share a drink. "Boys, let's strike a blow for liberty," he would say. One *Washington Post* reporter recalled, "It would have been very bad form to turn down old Cactus Jack. A man who refused a drink in those days was looked upon as a sissy, a slacker." Alice Roosevelt Longworth, wife of the Speaker of the House, calmly commented, that "No rumor could have exceeded the reality."

During a seven-month period toward the end of 1929, there were 934 speakeasies raided. The Justice Department paid as much as five dollars a day to the unemployed to act as informers. After this, protestors began to have their say against Prohibition. The Association Against the Prohibition Amendment distributed literature. The Prohibition Research Bureau parked their bus, named Diogenes, in front of the Capitol. They publicized that they would send the bus across the United States in search of ". . . the single individual who was a drunkard before national prohibition and who since has ceased drinking on account of the Eighteenth Amendment."[49]

On December 5, 1933, the Eighteenth Amendment was repealed and Prohibition ended. The first permit for a bar was given to the National Press Club. The Junior League Thrift Shop held the first Washington social event where liquor was legally served. During the previous 16 years, Washington had become a symbol for those who contended that a law against drinking could not be enforced. The heroes of the day were not followers of Francis Willard, founder of the WCTU; they were the famous bootleggers. In Washington, it was the Man in the Green Hat.

While one part of the city displayed its flamboyant behavior through ostentatious entertaining supported by bootlegged booze, another part of Washington developed quietly. During the first decades of the 20th century there was a "Secret City" within Washington, and the city's best-known musician, **Edward Kennedy Ellington**, came from there.

Within the Black community, there were strong class delineations. First, there were the aristocrats, perhaps 100 lawyers, doctors, bankers, and others descended from the wealthy old families. Next there were the middle class of perhaps 18,000 people whose occupations were centered around government and service. Most of this group took particular pride in their lighter skin and mulatto identification. Last, there was the lower class whose children's education rarely went as far as high school. In his autobiography, Ellington wrote, "I don't know how many castes of Negroes there were in the City at that time, but I do know that if you decided to mix carelessly with another you would be told that one just did not do that sort of thing. It might be wonderful for somebody, but not for me and my cousins."[50]

As a teenager, Eddie Ellington, was soon nicknamed "The Duke" because of his impeccable attire, his excellent manners, and his natural elegance. The attitudes of both of his parents greatly influenced his development. His mother, Daisy Kennedy, was the daughter of a police captain. He maintained that she taught him to believe in himself by telling him, "Edward, you are blessed. You don't have anything to worry about." [51]

Of his father, James E., he wrote, "J.E. always acted as though he had money, whether he had it or not. He spent and lived like a man who had money, and he raised his family as if he were a millionaire." Duke's father and uncle emigrated to Washington from Lincolntown, North Carolina, at the urging of their father. They worked as butlers to Dr. Middleton Cuthbert, a highly regarded society doctor. There James developed an aristocratic understanding of life. He passed his knowledge of good manners, good wine and food, and respect for each other on to his children. James later became a blueprint technician at the Navy Yard. A friend once said that, he had ". . . the speech of a Southern planter and the ability to strut even when sitting down."[52] Duke's sister Ruth recalled,

The house [1212 T St., Northwest] had a very large kitchen that led to a porch and garden. The dining room had French doors; there was a suite of mahogany furniture. My father kept the house as he had at Cuthbert's—cut glass and silver, with lace curtains in the living room. Every spring someone would come and pick up the carpets and replace them with rattan summer rugs, and take down the drapes and curtains and replace them with cloth shades.[53]

Duke grew up in a neighborhood of piano players, and at the insistence of his mother, he took a few lessons. Both of his parents played the piano. He remembered being moved to tears, as a child, by his mother's piano rendition of "The Rosary." She was a very religious woman, which also had a strong effect on his behavior and his music.

The Washington of his youth was a city where excellence was expected, and where people were inspired to work hard, have proper manners, and use good speech. Someone once described the atmosphere at the time in Washington for Blacks: "If a child couldn't eat in a certain restaurant, for example, because of segregation, perhaps the parent would tell him that only common people ate in restaurants, that nice people ate at home. Instead of having the developing ego damaged, the child would think that he was special."[54]

While he was still in high school, Duke's passion for baseball probably prompted him to take a job near Griffith Stadium in an ice cream parlor. When he was 14 years old, and home sick from school for a couple of weeks, he composed his first piece of music. He called it, "Soda Fountain Rag," perhaps inspired by his first job. He played a few of his melodies for friends, and his danceable tunes earned him a number of jobs at local parties. "I was invited to many parties where I learned that when you were playing the piano there was always a pretty girl standing down at the bass-clef end," he noted. His neighbor at the time, Mr. Pinn, remembered, however, "He'd plunk and plunk and plunk it out . . . two or three hours of plunking out the same chord or a few notes running away from it got to be pretty wearisome."[55] Later it was Mr. Pinn who helped Duke find his first big jobs.

During his last year in Armstrong High School, Duke won a National Association for the Advancement of Colored People poster contest, and he was awarded a scholarship to Pratt Institute in New York City to study art. Duke, however, chose to leave school and study music, although he was only one course shy of graduation. Years later, Armstrong High School awarded him an honorary degree. So did Howard University and many other national and international institutions.

Duke decided to study piano under his neighbor, Henry Grant, who was a high school music teacher. His long-time neighbor, friend, and sweetheart, Edna Thompson, a serious student of music, helped him learn to read sheet music. He married Edna in 1918. At the time, Duke was running a sign-painting business during the day and playing piano at night. When he made $10 one night on one job, he decided to place an ad in the phonebook. Soon he was making between $150 and $200 a week from bookings at the Industrial Cafe, Dreamland, Jack's, Mrs. Dyer's, Frank Holliday's, and Poodle Dog's. By 1920, Ellington's band, the "Washingtonians," were in demand in the city, and in 1923 Duke headed for New York.

A permanent position in New York's Cotton Club rocketed the Duke to stardom. He became known as "the man who made the Twentieth Century swing," and "the greatest single talent to be produced in the history of jazz." He proceeded to create a kingdom of music for himself. It was said that his favorite instrument was his orchestra. He called his band ". . . my expensive toy."[56]

As a performer, he was suave and sophisticated. Duke was a man of wit, taste, intelligence, and elegance. He also saw himself as a spoiled child. He was handsome and seductive, and he was prone to use phrases of endearment such as, "I love you madly!"

Duke was much more than a performer. He may have started out just having a good time and making lots of money, but in the course of his life, he discovered himself as a musician and composer. For the survival of his band, he developed his own style. One account relates how he would bring ideas to the recording studio as "scraps of melodies, harmonies and chord sequences." He and the band would alternate playing it until everybody had a version of it that was uniquely theirs. One pianist remembered, "What he does is like a chain reaction. Here's a section, here's a section and here's another and in between, he begins putting in the connecting links—the amazing thing about Ellington is that he can think so fast on the spot and create so quickly." Pieces would develop and individuals added harmonies. One trombonist commented, "I had to compose my own parts . . . you just went along and whatever you heard was missing, that's where you were."[57]

Duke was a manipulator of musicians. A musician ". . . might be needled by Duke's deliberate insults into showing what he could really do. There was a method behind the apparently chaotic undiscipline of the band."[58] He was dependent on his individual musicians; the various players and their moods dictated the music. This interdependence made his music a genuinely collective creation, which in turn, made the group "the greatest band in the history of jazz." One critic pointed out that this ". . . was music of professional entertainers of modest expectations, made in the community of night people with folk roots . . . Its major contribution to music was made in a social setting that no longer exists. It is difficult to imagine that a great musician of the future will be able to say, like one of Ellington's major soloists: 'All I wanted to be was a successful pimp, and then I found I could make it on the horn.' "[59]

"Ellington has been a name in music for about six decades of this century," observed Felix Grant, who has been involved in jazz music radio in Washington for nearly 40 years. "The only other person I cay say that is true of is Irving Berlin." Duke wrote popular songs such as "A-Train," "Sophisticated Lady," "Stormy Weather," "Satin Doll," and "Mood Indigo." He also composed for solo piano, bass duo, theater music, film scores, small and large jazz ensembles, jazz orchestras—alone and combined with symphonies—and liturgical works. Of the latter, Duke said, "You can jive with secular music, you can't jive with the Almighty."[60] Altogether, Duke is credited with more than 6,000 works.

Ellington gave the first nonclassical concert in Carnegie Hall in 1943. Perhaps that inspired some members of the Pulitzer Prize Committee to consider him for the award for music. In the 1950s, however, a few members of the board were not at all sure how to classify his music, and he was refused the honor. His comment was, "Fate is being kind to me. Fate doesn't want me to be too famous too young."[61] He was 66 years old.

The music of Ellington was world renowned. He played in Europe, Japan, Africa, South America, and the Soviet Union. On his 70th birthday, President Nixon held a dinner in his honor and presented him with the Presidential Medal of Freedom. He also received the French Legion of Honor and was elected to the Royal Swedish Academy of Music. In 1972, Yale University established the Duke Ellington Fellowship Fund, whose purpose is the perpetuation of traditional African-American music. In Washington, the Calvert Street Bridge was renamed for Duke Ellington, and the Duke Ellington School of the Arts was created for gifted young artists in the city.

Ellington worked 362 days a year, a co-worker once said. He never believed in retirement; he was driven by his music. When asked about his favorite piece of music, he gave the much-quoted response, "The next one. The one I'm writing tonight or tomorrow, the new baby is always the favorite."[62]

This combination of nurturing from an early age, of having high expectations set for him and a spiritual life for proper perspective, was not so difficult to provide," wrote columnist Courtland Milloy. "It sprung from the general belief among Black people that everybody was gifted in some way, and given the right push in the right place at the right time, the genius would always come through."[63]

Duke Ellington's legacy was much more that the music he left behind. Just days before he died in 1975, June Norton, a friend who had sung with his orchestra 40 years earlier, came to see him. "I thanked him," she said, "and told him I loved him. I said, 'Most people are contented to walk the earth, but you, you thrust your feet down and planted seeds for all the world.' He looked at me, grabbed my hands and kissed me."

Chapter 5

The World's Capital

I n the four decades following the Truman years, Washington developed into a modern city, unrecognizable to those who knew the city before World War II. A sense of rising prosperity came with the Republican administration under Eisenhower in the 1950s. The new buildings in downtown Washington stimulated rezoning of close-in residential areas for more office buildings. These buildings were needed to accommodate the multitude of new workers in both the private and public sectors. The gorgeous old late-19th-century mansions and homes disappeared one by one as land values escalated, as the economics of the times no longer justified their existence.

A mass exodus of Washington's white population in the 1950s was partly because of the enticement of the suburbs. The suburbs were fashionable, the houses were new, the schools were better, and the population was homogeneous. School integration in the city in 1954 accelerated these changes. For the first time, the racial balance in Washington was changing. The city had always counted between 20 and 35 percent of its population to be of African heritage. By 1970, that had changed to 70 percent.

Southwest Washington became part of an experiment called Urban Renewal. Some later renamed it urban removal. Whole neighborhoods were declared slum areas. Beginning in 1956, more than 4,500 buildings in Southwest Washington were bulldozed. Most of these houses were considered substandard, although they were just blocks from the Capitol. The concept of housing rehabilitation and restoration had been dismissed without discussion. Huge impersonal federal office buildings were built in the newly cleared areas. A freeway was constructed through the old Southwest neighborhood. Large, mundane, but not inexpensive, apartment complexes were constructed. The old residents were displaced with few places to go. Communities were broken apart, their churches and synagogues destroyed. Public housing complexes were constructed across the Anacostia River in Southeast, and those who could not afford to move anywhere else were relocated across the Anacostia River.

The Dupont Circle neighborhood, previously dominated by millionaires was also rezoned. All but two of the great palatial homes on the circle were replaced by mundane, functional office, commercial, or hotel structures. Aesthetics came to be interpreted through the eyes of economics. New buildings were good-looking only if they brought a profit to the developer and architect.

John F. Kennedy and his wife, Jacqueline, caused Washingtonians to reevaluate many of their recently conceived ideas in the 1960s. The old houses on Lafayette Square were ready to be torn down to make way for new office buildings. The old Corcoran Gallery across from the White House was also to be bulldozed. A new appreciation for history, however, was beginning to awaken in a few residents. Establishing a cultural center was an idea President Kennedy promoted. Although he did not live to see it, the Kennedy Center was opened and dedicated to him in 1972. There seemed to be a mad rush into the future.

This was also the beginning of increased transportation problems in the city. Streetcar service was ended in 1962, but the subway was not opened until 14 years later. Traffic problems escalated as more people became commuters. Washington was deserted in the evenings. The city had very few good restaurants, clubs, or theaters to attract locals to remain in town after hours. By the mid-1970s, a new generation of young, urban professionals began to make different demands on the city. They did not want to commute; rather they wanted to live in town and enjoy what the city offered.

In the late 1950s and early 1960s there was an influx of Blacks to Washington from rural areas, particularly the South. Some were well-educated, middle-class, professional people, but many were poorly educated, "refugees" seeking jobs and the psychological support of others. Dr. Martin Luther King, Jr.'s speech from the stairs of the Lincoln Memorial in 1963 brought hope to Blacks who were searching for a better life. Five years later, the situation had not radically improved, and when Dr. King was assassinated in 1968, the ensuing race riots caused suffering to both white-owned and minority-owned businesses. By the end of the 1960s, anti-Vietnam War protestors flowed into the nation's capital on a regular basis. Everyone seemed disillusioned with the city. Stable communities were broken up as fear drove away some of the last long-time residents, Black and white.

By 1968, Congress granted the residents the right to vote for the president and allowed a local government to be set up. Mayor Walter Washington was appointed as the first mayor. Later he became the city's first elected mayor. In the elections in 1976, Mayor Washington was defeated by Marion Barry for the Democratic nomination. Barry went on to win easily in the general election.

The Smithsonian Institution expanded significantly in the 1960s and 1970s. The National Museum of History and Technology (later renamed the National Museum of American History) opened in 1964. In the late-1960s, Joseph Hirshhorn gave his collection of contemporary art and sculpture to the Smithsonian. The next decade saw the opening of the National Air and Space Museum, the East Building of the National Gallery of Art, as well as the National Museum of American Art and the National Portrait Gallery. In 1987, the

collections of the Arthur M. Sackler Gallery and the National
Museum of African Art filled the new Smithsonian Quadran-
gle underground complex. Millions of tourists continued to
come to the city, which was becoming more conscious of the
importance of tourism to the local economy. A new convention Center lured large groups for meetings in the 1980s. New
luxury hotels mushroomed throughout the downtown sector
of the city. Neighborhoods began to take pride in their
uniqueness, offering festivals, parades, or special holiday
observances.

Confusion reigned during the Nixon, Ford, and Carter
years. Urban adventurers, who took advantage of low real
estate prices in some sections of the city, bought old homes
cheaply, painstakingly restored them, and then resold them
at a great profit. Historic preservation became popular. The
country's bicentennial celebration inspired many citizens
with a new appreciation of history. Groups banded together
to help save some of the landmark structures in Washington,
such as the Old Post Office building and the Willard Hotel on
Pennsylvania Avenue. Young professionals who had begun to
revitalize the city saw changes coming too slowly. Many with
children of school age soon realized the city's school system
was inadequate. They looked to private schools, or forsaking
their earlier optimistic convictions about the joys of urban
living, moved away.

The Reagan years lulled Washingtonians into a false sense
of security. Real estate values skyrocketed. Interest rates spi-
ralled, then fell. Property taxes multiplied geometrically. National attention focused on the nation's capital as its problems
associated with illegal drugs escalated. Crime statistics and
murder rates reached an unprecedented high. Even Mayor
Barry was not untouched by these problems.

Historically, the money makers of Washington have been
developers. In the 20th century, **Morris Cafritz** was the most
prolific. Cafritz came to the United States from Russia with
his family in 1908, when he was a teenager. The family moved
to Washington where his father started a grocery store near
24th and P Streets, Northwest. Morris worked there before

and after school and on Saturdays. On Sundays, he delivered newspapers.

The desire to start his own business in 1904 gave him the courage to ask his father for a loan of $1,400. With the money, he opened a wholesale coal yard at 4th and K Streets, Southwest. At the same time, he was managing a saloon near his father's shop. With some of the profits from his two businesses, he started an open-air theater showing silent movies to an audience sitting on chairs he set up in a vacant lot. The success of this seasonal enterprise led him to other businesses in the entertainment field.

A combined bowling alley and pool hall was his next venture. Located near to the Navy Yard, it did well. In 1910, he was told that one of the largest bowling establishments in the city was going to be put up for sale. The location, at 9th and G Streets, Northwest, seemed ideal. Cafritz jumped at the chance to buy it; soon he owned a chain of bowling alleys throughout the city. Washingtonians came to know him as the Bowling King.

Cafritz invested the profits from the alleys in real estate. The first properties he bought, in about 1918, were not far from one of the alleys, at 9th and K Streets, Northwest. In a short time, he sold the land for a fantastic profit of $40,000. Cafritz decided immediately that he ". . . wanted to get into something [a business] where the sky is the limit."[1]

By 1920, Cafritz owned a real estate office downtown. Recognizing the post-war need for good houses at moderate prices, he bought a golf course near his parents' home off Georgia Avenue, Northwest with borrowed money. He boasted he would build a thousand homes on the land. He named the new neighborhood Petworth, and he actually built more than two thousand homes there by the 1930s. He referred to the homes as ". . . family shrines, where the music of children's laughter and the peaceful contentment of domesticity are lived under the most ideal conditions."[2] The homes sold for $1,000 down on the $8,950 total price.

"I had no misgivings. I knew that if I built better homes than anyone else—and sold them at an appreciated price—

in a community which I could protect by the control of ownership—There could be no such thing as failure,"[3] wrote Morris Cafritz in 1925.

In the 1920s Cafritz concentrated on building houses, but he also built five major apartment houses and a few minor ones. He was undoubtedly influenced by the success of Harry Wardman. In 1923, he erected seven small apartment buildings on Spring Road, Northwest, whose names spelled out C-A-F-R-I-T-Z (the Cromwell, Aberdeen, Fernbrook, Rosedale, Islewood, Traymore, and Zeldwood). He borrowed this idea from the seven buildings Wardman built in 1914 which similarly spelled out W-A-R-D-M-A-N. Then, in 1926, he built the Corcoran Courts at 23rd and D Streets, Northwest, which he sold almost immediately for twice what it cost him to build.

The Cafritz Construction Company, which built all of Cafritz' houses, was employed by other developers as well. Some of Cafritz's early employees went on to be quite successful in their own right. Gustave Ring worked for Cafritz during the 1920s. In 1935, Ring obtained the first Federal Housing Administration loan in order to build the first garden apartment complex in the United States: Colonial Village, in Arlington, Virginia. Cafritz and Gustave Ring had joined forces five years earlier in 1930 to build the Westchester apartments on Cathedral Avenue, Northwest. The Depression permanently altered the original design, reducing the size of the complex by half. Despite the fact that it was never finished as planned, the Westchester held the title of the largest luxury apartment building in Washington for 20 years. It is still considered a prestigious place to live today.

Morris Cafritz was conservative with his money. When he realized that his Petworth homes had stopped selling in 1928, he quit building. The Depression caused him to curtail his construction business, but he managed to survive the lean years well. Afterwards, he was ready to begin building again when the economy improved. He was one of the few Washington businessmen to survive the Depression so well.

In the mid-1930s, Cafritz became the proponent of Art Deco style apartment buildings. He has been called the most successful builder of streamlined apartment houses. Many of his

Cafritz' Row House in Petworth

buildings, like the Gwenwood, built on 19th Street, North-west, had double doors at the entrance with round windows and glass-brick walls. He named the Gwenwood for his wife, Gwendolyn, when it was completed in 1939, as a birthday namesake present for her. It was made up of mainly efficiency apartments with Murphy beds and swing-down dining room tables.

Between 1925 and 1941, Cafritz erected more than 85 apartments. His sense of timing was unmatched. Not only could he predict where and when to build housing units, he also understood the importance of future development on K Street, Northwest as a new downtown business district. He was among the first to refashion the once-elegant residential street into a corridor of office buildings.

Decisions seemed to come easy to Morris Cafritz. When he saw a bargain in land, he bought it. The Temple Heights property on Connecticut Avenue, Northwest at Columbia Road became available in 1945 for $1 million in cash. Cafritz had one hour in which to make up his mind. He did not hesitate because he had tried to buy the same piece of property for $1.2 million 18 years earlier. It was another 12 years before Cafritz got around to building something on the land. "There was always something else to do. I have so much property in the Washington area, that if I lived to be a thousand, I wouldn't have it all built up."[4] Eventually, he did build the Universal Building and the Universal North Building on half the site, and he sold the rest to Hilton for the construction of the Washington Hilton Hotel.

For 30 years, Morris Cafritz kept the same office in a small suite in the Ambassador Hotel, which he had built in 1929. Years later, when he was asked why he didn't move into one of his luxurious new office buildings, he answered, "I couldn't afford the rent." His knowledge of land values contributed to his success as did his belief in his products. "The allurements of profit do not compare with the pride of having given to Washington a city of wonderful homes and happy owners,"[5] he said. He never retired from the business, and lived well into his eighties.

Morris Cafritz worked hard and felt he did not have the time to get married. Then Gwendolyn Detre de Surnay, a young Hungarian beauty, came into his life. She was the daughter of an internationally known Austro-Hungarian surgeon and immunologist, Dr. Laszlo Detre de Surnay, the co-developer of the Wasserman syphilis test. When Gwendolyn and Morris fell in love, they spent hours together riding horseback through Rock Creek Park. They were married in 1929; he was 46 years old and she was 20.

It was said Cafritz knew every lot in the city, and its worth. In 1939, he chose several lots on Foxhall Road, Northwest. There he built a fabulous mansion for his young wife who had strong social aspirations. While his home was being built, Cafritz stopped by nearly every day. One story he often told on himself, was that one day he reached across a fence to pick a few cherries from a tree in the next yard. He commented, "I certainly would like to have a tree like that on my own property." His foreman replied, "Mr. Cafritz, that *is* your property!"[6]

The Cafritz home contained 58 rooms, including a nightclub with a dance floor made of glass bricks lighted from below. Gwendolyn was as free with her husband's money as he was careful; he appreciated the way she enjoyed it. For 25 years their house was the center of social activity in Washington, and Gwendolyn was the center of attention at every party. Morris loved ballroom dancing and was prone to showing off his skills with his wife. Her parties lasted from the first one given in October to correspond with the opening of the Supreme Court session until everyone left town for the summer. Her rules for a party included having ". . . enough pretty women and clever men at your party, [so] then you can afford to invite a homely Cabinet officer and his wife." She added, "I always invite senators to my parties, but I seldom play around with the lower House." Her main rival on the Washington social scene was Pearl Mesta, the woman who was called "hostess with the mostest." The broadway play, "Call Me Madam!" was written about Pearl Mesta. When Gwendolyn was asked about inviting Pearl to one of her parties, she responded, "Darling, it won't be *that* big a party," and "Darling, I just couldn't bother with Mrs. Mesta; I go with girls my own age."[7]

Gwendolyn never discouraged media coverage and seemed to be constantly in the press. Cissy Patterson, owner of the *Washington Times-Herald*, featured her as "Beauty of the Week" in the 1940s. Later, Cissy assigned the top society writers to cover Gwendolyn Cafritz' parties, which made her almost as famous a personality as many of her guests. She possessed a regal air, ivory skin, ebony hair, dark eyes, and a 19-inch waist shown to best advantage in her Balmain, Dior, or Adolfo gowns. Her diamonds and jewels were almost as fabulous as the collection flaunted by her friend, Evelyn Walsh McLean, who was the last owner of the Hope diamond. Morris gave his wife $78,000 worth of jewelry for their 20th wedding anniversary in 1949. The collection was previously owned by the Drexels, a prominent Philadelphia family. It was sold to Cafritz at auction.

Gwendolyn Cafritz was forced to be a self-promoter, partly because of some of old Washington's prejudiced attitudes. She outraged Washington's "cavedwellers," a term used to describe the old, wealthy families who shunned any sort of publicity. Anyone might be invited to her dinner parties, and she was known to call the offices of Cabinet secretaries to inquire which days in the coming year might be free.

At first, Gwendolyn was considered rather comical, and there were many jokes about her. She regaled in some of these jokes. As a well-educated woman, she was known to play with the English language so much that many of her twisted phrases became known as "Gwendolynisms," which included, "I think it's nice to have a European background, if you come from Europe," and, "My dear, you look positively strategic!"[8]

One evening in 1964, while attending a banquet at the Homestead Hotel in Hot Springs, Virginia, Morris Cafritz quietly excused himself from the activities and went to his room. When a friend came to check on him, he had suffered a heart attack. Morris left an estate valued at $66 million, most of it in downtown office real estate investments. Today, such an estate would be valued at more than $1 billion. Morris willed half of his estate to the Cafritz Foundation, which he had set up years earlier. One quarter went to his widow, and the last quarter was divided equally among his three sons, all of whom became involved in real estate and development in Washington.

When Gwendolyn died in 1988, the portion of the estate left to her by her husband had grown to be valued at about $84 million. Of that, $63 million was left to the Morris and Gwendolyn Cafritz Foundation. She also left the foundation all her personal property, whose value may have exceeded $90 million. Her three sons filed several lawsuits to overturn her will and to divide her personal property and her marital trust property among themselves. The bitter fight has continued into the 1990s with no resolution. The sons and their mother were never known to be close. They were raised under the supervision of servants. When she was asked once about the fact that their names all began with a "C" (Calvin, Carter, and Conrad), she said, "Morris names all children, horses, dogs, apartments houses and everything around. I just make speeches."[9]

When Morris Cafritz died, he left two legacies. First, he and Gwendolyn remain among the greatest philanthropists in Washington during the 20th century. The Cafritz Foundation contributes millions of dollars each year to local organizations involved in the arts, humanities, community service, education, and health. It is Washington's largest local charity. Second, he literally made the modern city of Washington what it is today. By 1964, he had built homes for 20,000 Washingtonians, and was responsible for the construction of more than 10 percent of all the privately held commercial office space in downtown Washington. "He just wanted to build, build, build!" said a friend. "He always had a new job going."[10]

The press has always been a power in Washington. Cissy Patterson used the *Times-Herald* to express her opinions. Gwen Cafritz used the local newspapers to gain prestige. **Katharine Meyer Graham** took control of *The Washington Post* and became one of the most powerful people in Washington.

Stilson Hutchins had started *The Washington Post* in 1877. Eugene Meyer, a millionaire, bought it in 1933 at a bankruptcy sale from Edward B. (Ned) McLean. Meyer poured money into the *Post* for 20 years in an effort to keep it afloat. One of his daughters, Katharine, showed an early interest in journalism. When she was just out of college in 1939, the *San Francisco News* gave her a job paying $21 a week. She stayed for seven months. Recognizing his daughter's talents, Meyers offered her a job at the *Post* in the Letters to the Editor department, paying $25 a week. She took the job editing incoming letters. She also began writing editorials. Alice Roosevelt Longworth remembered Meyers saying, "You watch my little Kate; she'll surprise you." He later wrote a friend, "Kate's the only one [of his five children] like me. She's got a hard mind. She'd make a great businessman."[11]

During her first year at the *Post*, she wrote 103 editorials. She also met Philip Graham who came to Washington to clerk for Supreme Court Justice Reed. Katharine and Philip were married in 1940. When Katherine suggested that perhaps she should stay home and learn to cook, Philip responded, "My God. I don't think I could stand having you wait around with a pie for me to come home from the Court. You continue to work and we'll pay a maid with what you make."[12]

In 1943, Philip joined the Army Air Corps, and the couple moved to South Dakota, and later to Pennsylvania. Of their four children, two were born during World War II. "I really felt I was put on earth to take care of Phil Graham," Katharine wrote. "He was so glamorous that I was perfectly happy just to clean up after him. I did all the scutwork: paid the bills, ran the house, drove the children. I was always the butt of family jokes. You know, good old Mom, plodding along. And I accepted it. That's the way I viewed myself."[13]

The relationship between Philip Graham and Katharine's father was a close one. Before Graham went into the Army, Meyer asked him if he would be interested in taking control of the paper. On January 1, 1946, Meyer transferred the voting stock to Graham as a sale; however, because Graham did not have much money, Meyer gave him a gift of $75,000 to pay for most of the stock. In 1954, Graham bought the *Times-*

Washington Post Building—1893

Herald, which was a turning point in the financial success of the paper. Later, he bought *Newsweek.* He also optimistically invested in a television station in Jacksonville, Florida.

Graham prevailed upon his wife to write "The Magazine Rack" column in the *Post,* a Sunday digest of current magazine articles, but she still stayed in the background. One acquaintance described her as, ". . . having a nervous manner and [being] smothered by her husband."[14] In 1957, Philip Graham suffered a nervous breakdown, and Katharine concentrated her efforts on taking care of him. In 1963, Philip died from a self-inflicted shotgun blast. "When my husband died I had three choices," Katharine wrote, "I could sell it [The *Post*]. I could find somebody else to run it. Or I could go to work. And that was no choice at all. I went to work . . . it was simply inconceivable to me to dismantle all that my father and my husband had built with such labor and such love."[15]

Three days later, she addressed the *Post*'s board of directors. One editor remembered, "She sat there looking ashen, dressed in black, her eyes downcast. Then she looked up and in a low but level voice began to speak."[16] She told the gathered assemblage of editors, lawyers, and executives that no part of the company would be sold. The next day, some of the most powerful men and women in Washington came to the Washington Cathedral for Philip Graham's funeral service, including President Kennedy, Robert Kennedy, Felix Frankfurter, Stuart Symington, and Alice Roosevelt Longworth.

Katharine Graham became president of *The Washington Post* upon the death of her husband. "I had to use the Montessori method—learn by doing," she commented. "My worst moments were the public appearances. Speeches and interviews were the hardest thing for me to learn; I wasn't very articulate." She found walking into a world of men inhibiting. "I had deferred to men for ages. They *knew* better," Katharine noted, "I really didn't understand what was going on when I was condescended to, which was both good and bad. It was bad in the sense that it was rather stupid, but it was good in the sense that I wasn't paranoid about how I was being treated."[17]

A number of experienced friends came to her aid, such as Robert McNamara, Joseph Alsop, and James Reston. Reston asked, "Don't you want to leave your children a greater news-paper than you inherited?" Walter Lippmann encouraged her and advised, ". . . make a note of the stories in the papers that interest you . . . call in the reporter and have him explain it to you . . . I wouldn't try to worry out everything myself."[18]

As the new president of the *Post*, Katharine Graham was the first to acknowledge how shy and self-conscious she was. Her children couldn't believe that she had to practice saying "Merry Christmas." Her close friends were surprised about these traits since they knew she had the nerve to tell people off when she felt they deserved it. It was her willingness to learn, together with an abundance of energy and determination, that brought her through the early years at the paper. She knew she would have to educate herself.

Straightaway, Katharine attacked her own weaknesses. "I think it's stupid not to try to learn something you have to do, and I recognized that I would have to give speeches." She hired a speech coach. She was also terrified of flying, but she wrote, ". . . you can't live not flying, so I flew." Worst of all, she realized that ". . . ideas everybody else had learned in business school would come to me as new. It was a pain in the neck for people around me." She also had to create a new image since she had been disparagingly described as "dowdy" and "dumpy." A friend took her aside one day and said, "Look, I'm going to tell you something. You can't look like this!" She began having her clothes made, and carefully chose a hairdresser. Katharine wrote a friend, "There is no recovery really from grief—even the void left by having to take care of someone who isn't well; but after some time passes, you become someone else."[19]

In 1965, the *Post* felt the first major change under its new president. "It was pretty clear something had to be done," she said about the somewhat aimless editorship of her friend, Alfred Friendly. "As much as I loved Al, I could see management decisions in the city room not being made. But it was extremely difficult [to make the change] . . . Al was hurt, but he went abroad [for the *Post*] and won a Pulitzer."[20]

In 1965, Benjamin Bradlee was the editor of *Newsweek*. Katharine Graham called him to Washington as a possible replacement for Al Friendly. He was dynamic and unaffected;

she was impressed by his ambitions for the paper. When he joined the *Post*, he was told to expect the editorship in a year or two. Three months later, he gained complete control. Katharine and Ben's mutual support and respect have become almost legendary.

In 1971, The Washington Post Company stock went public with the blessings of Katharine Graham. When *Post* editors and Wall Street commentators expressed negative remarks about the public stock offerings, she responded,

> One hears a certain amount of conversation about whether our commitment to journalistic excellence and integrity is consistent with our commitment to profitability. I can assure you . . . you cannot have one without the other . . . I'm afraid that on Wall Street they think all I'm after is prizes and ego trips; that how the stock does doesn't matter to me. Half of them think I don't work at all and just go to parties; the other half think I'm obsessed with Watergate . . . I get a lot of flak at the *Post*, too, when I talk about profitability. They get pretty tight at the mention of M-O-N-E-Y; they think I'm some heartless bitch. I have to do an endless song and dance about how excellence and profitability go hand in hand—which isn't an act. I really think they do. It costs plenty to put two people on a story for sixteen months, and profit-making *is* my priority. If it weren't, I goddamn well shouldn't be here.[21]

In 1975, the *Post*'s union contract with the pressmen ran out and a bitter strike ensued. Presses stopped and some were sabotaged. The strike lasted more than four months. To keep the paper on the streets, management personel worked double shifts as production crews. The strike was settled and Katharine Graham gained new respect from her peers.

More than any other event in the history of the *Post*, the Watergate Scandal in 1972, which ended in the resignation of President Nixon, brought Katharine Graham into the world spotlight. The Watergate story dragged on for months after the Democratic headquarters in the Watergate Hotel had been broken into by burglars associated with the Committee to Reelect the President. The story was a risky one, but Ben

Bradlee gave Katharine constant reassurance. When her friend Henry Kissinger warned her of the political ramifications of her actions, she described the moment as "blood-chilling." She received a ridiculously crude threat from former attorney general, John Mitchell. Her support of the reporters and editors involved did not falter; it helped complete the image of her as one of Washington's most powerful women.

Although many people still think of Katharine Graham as a confidante of Presidents and a fabulous party-giver, she would prefer to be thought of as a publisher and business-woman. She was the first women chief executive officer in a *Fortune 500* company. A respected publisher once said, "The record shows that over the past twenty years she had made virtually all the key business decisions right."[22]

The demise of the *Evening Star* in 1981 brought near complete power to the *Post* in the Washington market. When Eugene Meyer bought *The Post* in 1933, it was bottom on the list of five local papers. Fifty-seven years later, it is on top. Katharine Graham is one of the nation's most influential women. Every president since Kennedy (except Nixon) has been invited to her home and has accepted. Her son, Donald, now publisher of *The Washington Post*, commented, "As in the rest of my life, my mother has given me everything but an easy act to follow."[23]

One decidedly impossible act to follow in Washington was that of **J. Edgar Hoover**, Director of the Federal Bureau of Investigation. He felt no one could ever take his place. Under Hoover's direction, the bureau became a one-man operation, and it was nearly impossible to speak of Hoover without mentioning the FBI.

Hoover, a lifelong resident of Washington, was born on New Year's Day, 1895. He lived with his mother in her Capitol Hill house at 415 Seward Square, Southeast, until she died. The house was torn down in 1965 to make way for the Capitol Hill Methodist Church. Hoover lived the rest of his life in a Northwest Washington house. He never married; everyone knew his only true love was the FBI.

As a young lawyer in 1917, J. Edgar Hoover entered the Department of Justice, serving as an assistant attorney general. The Bureau of Investigation, at that time, was just a small, nine-year-old division of the department. By 1924, Attorney General Harlan Fiske Stone decided that the bureau should be more efficient, and that it should serve as a cooperative clearinghouse for crime-solving throughout the nation. Stone had several other ideas; however, he knew that the first step was finding a strong leader for the bureau.

Stone's inquiries concerning a capable man to fill the post of bureau director led him to Hoover, whose executive abilities were highly recommended. Attorney General Stone and the 29-year-old J. Edgar Hoover had extensive talks about the bureau's current problems, the changes that needed to be made, and the standards that must to be set up for the future.

Hoover immediately moved with confidence into his position as the bureau's acting director, and, in almost no time, he was appointed director. He eliminated any man from the bureau whose character was the least bit suspicious. He then appointed intelligent, well-educated men to fill the vacant positions. He built up morale in the bureau and created a productive organization for investigating crime in the United States.

Throughout the 1930s, the bureau's criminal jurisdiction was greatly enlarged under Hoover's control. It became a federal offense to cross state lines to avoid prosecution for burglary, rape, murder, and other crimes. Also during this time, special agents were given the right to make arrests and carry weapons. By 1935, the Bureau of Investigation was renamed as the Federal Bureau of Investigation.

Publicity was important to J. Edgar Hoover, who constantly romanced the press. Newspaper headlines about horrible crimes involving gangsters and kidnappings across the country were turned around by Hoover into success stories for the FBI. He established the "Ten-Most-Wanted List." Posters with pictures of these criminals were sent to every federal post office by the FBI. Hoover even reached out to a generation of children by encouraging the sale of G-man toys, books, and games. By the early 1950s tours of the FBI facility in Washington were offered to visitors. Today, the FBI tours are among the most popular in the nation's capital.

As J. Edgar Hoover gained power in the FBI, those who served under him became somewhat powerless in his presence. Many seemed to look upon him as omnipotent, and he encouraged this type of thinking. He became a living legend in his time, so much so that humorist-writer Art Buchwald once wrote in his syndicated newspaper column that perhaps J. Edgar Hoover was just a mythical person who did not really exist, except in *Reader's Digest*.

There were many FBI employees who could not have been more loyal. They saw him as a paragon of virtue. These same loyal servants, however, often proved to be the downfall of others who dared to express any concern about Hoover's abilities or decisions. Disloyalty was career death in the FBI under Hoover. They said Hoover's ears were everywhere. All employees had to be above suspicion of even tolerating disrespect from others, or punishment would be handed down. Punishment could be a simple passing-over of an expected raise, or it could even be an immediate transfer to a field office in Butte, Montana, or Anchorage, Alaska.

Hoover's one close associate was Clyde Anderson Tolson, who was five years younger than Hoover. Tolson joined the FBI in 1928 after serving as private secretary to three different secretaries of war. Not much is known about Tolson, except that he was always at Hoover's side, taking notes and whispering in his ear. He was Hoover's confidential secretary, and the only man in the bureau to call him Eddie.

Tolson and Hoover lunched together every day at the Mayflower Hotel when they were not travelling. Their trips were scheduled on a regular basis. The two men always travelled to New York to inspect the New York field office over New Year's Day, which was Hoover's birthday. In late January they went to inspect the Miami field office, and in August they went to inspect the San Diego field office. Only under threat of great punishment did anyone ever infer that Hoover and Tolson might be enjoying their visits to these places.

Hoover was known as *the Director* by those who worked for him. Questioning anything Hoover said was strictly taboo. One incident recorded Hoover's welcoming a class of new agents into the FBI. He personally shook hands with the new agents as he carefully and quickly scrutinized each man. Then he turned to one of their counselors and said that one agent was a "pinhead" and should be gotten rid of. Those who were given the ominous task of discovering and dismissing the offensive agent, did not know Hoover's definition of a pinhead, but they were not going to ask. They could loose their job for such an inquiry. It was suggested that they check the hats of each new agent. Perhaps Hoover meant that one agent's head was too small. Those with the smallest hat size were singled out. Unfortunately, there were three who wore exactly the same size small hat, so just to be safe, all three were fired by the counselors.

In another story, one agent lost control of himself under pressure one day, and blurted out that Hoover was a "senile old son of a bitch." His superior noted the remark in a report sent to Hoover. Fortunately, the report was intercepted before it reached its destination at headquarters, and the following phrase was added: ". . . psychiatry obviously required. Shock must have temporarily deranged him." The agent did undergo psychiatric examinations but, with careful editing of the final mental health report indicating that the frustration came about because of ". . . being unable to meet the Director's high standards of performance,"[24] the man's job was saved.

The "Fat Boys" campaign was instituted by Hoover in the 1950s. Some said it was because Hoover had lost weight and then felt that all agents should benefit from the feeling of well-being he gained by his experience. Another source alludes to a letter from a Canadian lady received by Hoover. The subject was the agents on the shooting range during the FBI tour. Their posteriors were described by the lady as being much larger than those of the Royal Canadian Mounties!

The weight program was always a top priority with Hoover. All agents were judged against a chart furnished by the Metropolitan Life Insurance Company. One pound over the maximum for your height and frame could mean the denial of a promotion or worse. Creating illusions of thinness were raised to an art form. One agent wore an oversized suit.

Another claimed that he was not overweight; he was just too short. The program is still in effect today, and the idea of being placed on the "Fat Boy" program can bring fear into the mind of an otherwise very brave, although slightly overweight, man.

Going to see Hoover could be a dangerous undertaking. It was said that anything might happen in Hoover's office. He was not a tall man, and many claimed that his desk and chair were raised to give the illusion of height. Also, the chair provided for the visitor seemed to have a cushion that deflated the longer one sat in it. The experience was once compared to making one ". . . feel like a stork trying to sit in a water bucket."[25] Also, Hoover was the only person in the bureau allowed to use blue ink. That way, whenever he wrote a note, everyone immediately recognized it by the color of the ink.

Hoover's little idiosyncrasies became well known and increased proportionately with his years at the bureau. All agents asked to act as Hoover's chauffeurs were strictly instructed to make sure the car they drove was immaculate, inside and out. They were also told never drive above the speed limit or make any left turns. This last demand made routing across any city particularly difficult. The reason behind the rule came from an accident Hoover was involved in. The driver of Hoover's car once made a routine left turn and another car struck it just behind the driver's door where Hoover was sitting. From then on, there were no more left turns made when Hoover was riding in the car to avoid ever having another such accident.

When Hoover travelled, he wanted all his hotel arrangements made in advance. He always got a suite of rooms, including a living room and two bedrooms with separate baths for himself and Tolson. All appliances had to have neatly typed operating instructions attached to them. Flowers were placed in the living room only. Two identical packets of information were provided, one in each bedroom, to give information on the place he was visiting, including maps and brochures on the history and commerce of the area. He also insisted on having four down pillows on each bed. For Tolson, he wanted a bottle of 8-year-old Grant Scotch whiskey, and for himself, Jack Daniels, black label. The ice cubes were not to be thin, but fat ones so as not to melt too fast.

In a practice that would never be accepted today, Hoover had bureau employees work on his house when something needed to be repaired. Once, when a light bulb burned out, Hoover became so upset a decision was made to replace every bulb in the house twice a month to avoid having any burn out.

Hoover worked at the bureau until he died of a heart attack in May 1972. His body lay in state in the Rotunda of the Capitol. Chief Justice Earl Warren read the eulogy. Hoover chose to be buried in Congressional Cemetery in Southeast Washington with his parents. A few years later, when Tolson died, he was buried almost next to Hoover. Hoover left the FBI as his legacy, and his "monument" is the FBI headquarters building, which was named for him after his death. It is said to be the ugliest building in town; even Hoover called the building's design obnoxious, and said "It looked like something from Mars."[26]

Just a few blocks from the J. Edgar Hoover FBI building on Pennsylvania Avenue is the National Theater where another Washingtonian, a contemporary of Hoover's, discovered what her life's work would be. **Helen Hayes**, who has become known across the country as America's "First Lady of Theater," started her acting career at the age of five, in Washington in 1905.

Helen's parents were Irish Catholics, and she attended the local Catholic schools. She also attended Miss Minnie Hawks' Dancing School. Her debut came during the May Ball. "Miss Hawks, I believe, thought I was too clumsy to dance with the rest of the pupils," reminisced Helen Hayes, "so she allowed me to do my specialty, which was impersonating well-known people."[27]

A New York theatrical producer was in the audience that night. He invited Helen's mother to bring her to New York. They went four years later, and Helen made her New York debut at the age of nine. She came back to Washington to finish school and worked with the Columbia Players in the city during the summers. Then in 1916, she starred in the New York production of *Pollyanna*. Years later, she said, "Once I thought the theater had robbed me of the richness of life—no childhood, no adolescence, no parties, no football games. But I know the theater has repaid me a hundred-fold."[28]

Helen had the opportunity to tour the country with acting companies as a child. There were some towns, however, that prohibited such companies from employing child performers. "And one of them was my own home town. Every time we came to Washington," said Helen, "I had to be replaced by midgets."[29] She did not play at the National Theater until she was 18 years old.

Helen Hayes is among the first to admit to shyness. "I was pushed on the stage by my mother, but the theater became my own choice as the years went on,"[30] Helen recalled. She began to gain courage, and although she was terribly self-conscious in social situations, she wooed the world on stage. Acting was hard work, but Helen saw it as a job, a delightful job. She was sincere in her performances and she attempted to understand each character she played.

The approval Helen sought was not found in monetary rewards, but in human recognition. Helen's priorities have always been in happiness and good relationships, not money. A number of actors and actresses took her under their wing, including Lillian Russell. In 1928, she met Charles MacArthur, the playwright. Helen said that the bravest act of her life was speaking to him first. They were at a party, and he had a bag of peanuts in his hand. She simply asked, "What are you eating?" The reply has become an often told story in her life. "Peanuts," he said as he handed the bag to Helen, "I wish they were emeralds." At first, Charles said he was infuriated that Helen had told that story on him. He had the last laugh, however, when he served in Burma during World War II. He bought a bag of inexpensive, uncut emeralds and carried them back home to give to her, saying, "Emeralds, I wish they were peanuts."[31]

They were married in 1928. On her wedding day, she received many gifts from people she called famous strangers. One came from Harpo Marx. It was a Steinway piano crate filled with gardenias. Although many people felt their marriage would not last, Helen and Charles were very happy together until his death 32 years later. Helen said of husband, "He released me from my cocoon and sent me flying out into life." He was a writer and Helen claimed she went to Hollywood just to be with him. "I'd give up my stage life any day to keep my husband and my home," she once said, ". . . and I'm thankful I don't have to choose . . . and that he is in sympathy with my work."[32] Of Helen, Charles said, "Sometimes I feel I've domesticated an angel."[33]

They had one daughter, Mary, and later adopted a son, James. When Helen became pregnant with Mary in 1929, she had to leave the production in which she was starring on the advice of her doctor. The show was canceled. The remaining actors and actresses sued the producer for the four unplayed weeks of the show. He denied that he owed them anything, claiming that the show was canceled because of the baby, which was an act of God. He lost the suit, but Helen's baby became known as the "Act-of-God" baby because of all the publicity surrounding the case.

When the child first smiled, Helen rushed the baby to Hollywood so that Charles could see his daughter's happy face. He was cynically inspired by that open demonstration of motherly affection to write a play. It centered on a sinful mother who clings to her child until death. It was called, *The Sin of Madelon Claudet*. The play was made into a movie in 1931. Helen had the starring role, but she refused to go to the opening night preview. As this was her first movie role, she felt her screen image must be terrible. For this portrayal, however, she won her first Academy Award.

Both of Helen's children made their stage debuts in the Washington suburb of Olney, Maryland. James went on to become a well-known actor. He starred in the popular television program of the 1970s, *Hawaii-Five-O*. In 1949, her daughter, Mary, was just becoming a professional actress when she was stricken with polio and died at the age of 19. Helen decided to retire from acting, but within just a few years, she was convinced to come back to the movies and stage. "I've always been talked into things," she said. Then in 1956, Charles died. By that time, James was married and had his own life. Helen decided that there was really no other option for her than going back to work.

The year before Charles died, she celebrated her 50th anniversary on the stage. She commented in a matter-of-fact way on the event by saying, "I never even thought about it. Somebody remembered I made my debut at the age of 5 and figured out that I was 55 last month, and all of a sudden I was a living monument." In New York, in 1955, a Broadway playhouse was named for her and she said, "An actress' life is so transitory—[then] suddenly you're a building."[34]

Helen Hayes' list of accomplishments is much too long to compile. She was a radio star and named radio's favorite actress in 1937 and she won the Jefferson Award in recognition of her much later performances on the radio. The theater's Tony Award was given to her in 1947. She starred in many movies, including *A Farewell To Arms* and *Anastasia*. In 1970, she won a second Oscar for her role as best-supporting actress in the movie *Airplane*. Helen was also honored as 1973's *Woman of the Year* and, in 1978, as *American Woman of the Century*. Helen wrote four best-selling books and has been granted 51 honorary degrees, including a Doctor of Fine Arts from The Catholic University of America in Washington. She has a special place in her heart for the university and has given many performances there to help raise money for a new theater.

Forty years later, Helen Hayes continues to give back. In 1983, the Helen Hayes Award was established by the American Theater Awards Society to ". . . recognize achievement in theatrical productions and performances, promoting excellence in the theatrical profession in Washington." Not only has she lent her name to the award, she has also attended every award ceremony. "Well, the theater is tough, it is hard. You either come out discouraged or belonging. But if you belong, there is no more enriching experience for anyone,"[35] she said.

Someone once said, Helen Hayes has the capacity to make people feel special. She never seems to quit. She explained in the early 1970s:

And though I've retired umpteen times, I find it so ex-
hausting that I always come back to the theater . . . I won't
stop work . . . I'm a compulsive worker, always have been
. . . Charlie used to rail me about this because he always
tried to get out of things while I was always getting into
them. 'Of course I'll outlive you and your wasted energy,'
he said, 'and on your tombstone I'll put "god called Helen
and she couldn't say no.' "[36]

Another person in Washington's history who just could not
say no was **Marion S. Barry**. He has been described as the
most powerful figure in the nation's capital during the past
100 years. For a quarter of a century, Barry threw himself into
city politics. He was resourceful, methodical, and a hard
worker who believed he was invincible.

"Some people are destined and some people are determined, and I am determined,"[37] Barry was known to say.
From a early age, he proved he was going to succeed. He was
born in the small Mississippi town of Itta Bena. His father,
Marion S. Barry, Sr., was a handyman who died when Barry
was 4 years old. His mother, Mattie, moved to Memphis
where she worked as a domestic. Barry grew up in the segregated city of Memphis during the 1940s and 1950s. He never
forgot or forgave the inequality of treatment he received in
his youth.

Early in his life, Barry found that money brought him a
certain kind of respect. A story is told of how Barry earned
extra money to buy his first really nice suit. While escorting
his two younger stepsisters to school, he would pause with
them for a while, on a streetcorner where the girls sang songs
to attract passersby. Barry collected the small change people
gave in appreciation for the entertainment, and then added it
to the money he earned bagging groceries, delivering newspapers, and waiting tables.

As a teenager, Barry proved to be an achiever when he
became the first Black Eagle Scout in Memphis in the 1950s.
He collected merit badges the way other boys collected
stamps. He was a good student in high school, but he also
found time to shoot dice and earn a little money for a bottle
of wine to share with his pals. He wanted to be accepted,

however, he also wanted to be noticed and to be known as different.

Five predominately Black colleges accepted Barry's applications. After some consideration, he chose to attend LeMoyne College in Memphis. While Barry was in college he adopted a middle name, since like his father, his middle initial, S, stood alone and represented no name. He read a newspaper story in which the name Shepilovk was mentioned. Barry chose this to be his middle name, Marion Shepilovk Barry. Over the years, however, he has reverted to the name he was born with.

Barry served as vice president of the student government and treasurer of the senior class. He also became president of the school's chapter of the National Association for the Advancement of Colored People. His radical behavior began to surge to the forefront when he was nearly expelled for writing a letter demanding the resignation of a member of the school's board of trustees. Barry took as a personal insult the statement made by the man concerning segregation on the city's buses.

In 1958, Barry was graduated from LeMoyne College and went on to attend Fisk University in Nashville, where he earned a master's degree in chemistry. Choosing a career as a research chemist appealed to Barry, perhaps because it gave him a way to prove that he was no less a student or worker than those he felt were his oppressors. Perhaps, it was his methodical thinking, which is so much a part of the study of chemistry. Later, his political career would succeed because of his ability to think methodically through each step of a given process to produce the desired results.

While at Fisk, in the early 1960s, Barry became active in the civil rights movement. He became the compromise winner as first chairman of the Student Nonviolent Coordinating Committee (SNCC) because the local leader was not in the room when the vote was taken. After five months, he stepped down, deciding to begin to his doctoral studies in chemistry, which he never finished.

In March 1962 Barry married a young woman he had only recently met, Blantie Charlesetta Evans. When they were married, he told her, "You hang with me, you'll be a First Lady."[38] Two years later, Barry left her. According to the divorce suit filed in 1969, he disappeared and abandoned her, leaving her impoverished. In one interview Blantie stated that she realized they were too different to make it together.

The SNCC attracted Barry to New York City and then to Washington where the city's SNCC operation was in need of leadership. The "Free DC Movement" in 1965 brought local attention to Barry, who was guiding the movement in Washington and advocating home rule. Donations were solicited from local businesses under the threat of boycott if they refused to donate their fair share. By 1968, Barry was recognized as a radical. He was organizing "mancotts" (boycotts) of buses in protest of fare increases, and declaring that Blacks were at war with "The Man." He even predicted the riots of the 1960s by demanding that white-owned businesses in the ghetto turn over 51 percent of the ownership to Blacks or they would burn.

Barry met frequently with U.S. Secretary of Labor William Wirtz in 1967 to discuss the problems of poorly educated and unemployed Black youths in Washington. He convinced Wirtz to allocate $300,000 for a project called Youth Pride, Inc. Thousands of inner-city Black children were put to work cleaning streets, painting buildings, and landscaping in the city. Barry and a friend from Fisk University, Mary Treadwell, gained full control of the Youth Pride, Inc. business. They married in 1972. Six years later, they separated; their divorce was finalized in 1982. Not long after her separation from Barry, Treadwell was indicted for looting federal funds from Youth Pride, Inc. Barry came out unscathed, although Mary Treadwell's sister, father, future third husband, and 13 others were indicted. Treadwell was convicted, fined, and jailed.

Barry's political career in Washington began in 1970 when he was elected to a police advisory board. One year later, he won a seat on the D.C. School Board. In 1974, he won one of four at-large seats on the D.C. City Council, and he was reelected in 1976. By 1978, Barry wanted to be mayor. Washington had received home rule in 1968, and Walter Washington had been appointed to serve as Washington's first mayor.

Later, when elections were held, he was overwhelming elected as mayor. Barry, Walter Washington, and Sterling Tucker competed for the Democratic nomination. Barry won 34 percent of the vote. He won the mayoral election against Republican Arthur Fletcher in a landslide.

In 1982, Barry ran again for mayor and won; in 1986, he was elected again. By this time arrogance was beginning to rule Barry's speech and actions. He called himself, "Mayor for Life," and insisted that even his friends call him Mr. Mayor, or at least, "M.B." or "Boss." Barry adopted the habit of referring to himself in the third person when giving interviews. Some have tried to explain his political philosophy as one in which he cultivated rather than cut off, his enemies. He enjoyed outthinking his political enemies, and then giving the appearance of truly liking them so that they would be forced to pretend they liked him. In this way, he was always in control.

Barry became a hero to many whose backgrounds were rooted in poverty. He also became the darling of city developers because he promoted new building projects on downtown properties. He was called the "Prince of Power." His every movement gave off a sense of domination. He walked with a hallmark strut, his chin upturned, his lips pursed, and his eyes penetrating anything that came under his glare. Over the years, Barry was often under scrutiny for his personal conduct. He seemed to enjoy placing himself in questionable situations, and then adopting a "catch-me-if-you-can" attitude. Always, he vehemently denied all accusations ranging from political corruption to illegal drugs.

Barry was often compared to a cat with nine lives. His first altercation with the D.C. police came on May 13, 1969. A policeman was ticketing his car, which was illegally parked outside the Youth Pride, Inc. headquarters. The officer reported that Barry rushed out and yelled, "If you put a ticket on my car . . . I'll kill you."[39] He then tore up the ticket and threw it into another officer's face. He hit one of the policemen and tore his shirt. A scuffle ensued. Three Youth Pride employees became involved in the fight. All were taken to court. The codefendant were acquitted, but the jury was hung on its verdict over Barry. He learned then the power just one juror can have, one who would ardently support him.

Over the years that Barry served as mayor, eleven of his top aides, including two former deputy mayors, Ivanhoe Donaldson and Alphonse G. Hill, were sent to prison on charges usually centering on misuse of their offices and extortion of federal funds. The mayor's response to this was that the Black man was unfairly pursued by prosecutors. He has always claimed that he has been ". . . hounded, harassed, vilified [and] slandered."[40]

The 1990 trial of Marion Barry on federal charges of illegal drug use and perjury brought international attention to Washington's mayor and embarrassment to the nation's capital and the country. To the end, Barry refused to accept any blame for his actions, the repercussions of which will be felt for many years to come. He said, *"They* did it to me." Before the trial began, he said, "What's the worst they could say, that I used cocaine with them . . . most Washingtonians . . . they may think I may have done that . . . So if I testify I'd used cocaine before, that's not damaging. People already think that." After many in the community expressed their disappointment in the example Barry has set for their children, he commented, "I may be a poor role model, but . . . being a poor role model is not a crime."[41] When he was confronted about lying about his chemical dependency, he stated, "That was the disease talking. I did not purposely do that to you. I was a victim."[42] Knowing the power of a hung jury, Barry said, "In this town, all it takes is one juror saying, 'I'm not going to convict Marion, I don't care what you say.' "[43]

The legacy Marion Barry had hoped to leave behind, one of himself as a civil rights fighter and outstanding politician for two decades, is now overshadowed by the city's high murder rate of mostly young Black men, the trial, and the videotape of the mayor smoking crack cocaine with a former girlfriend, Rasheeda Moore, in the Vista Hotel. The tape, shown on national television, recorded Barry's arrest by FBI agents and his retort, which became the most repeated expression of the trial: "Bitch set me up!" In fact, columnist Tony Kornheiser suggested entering the statement in a contest for a new city slogan.

The Barry trial became a sensational one, dividing the city into supporters and antagonists. After eight weeks of testimony and deliberation, the trial ended with his conviction on one count of cocaine possession, one acquittal, and 12 counts not resolved because of a hung jury. When Judge Thomas Penfield Jackson handed down sentencing, he said he based his decision to imprison Barry on the belief that Barry was guilty of crimes beyond drug possession as exhibited by the government prosecutors. The judge later said, "I am not happy with the way the jury addressed the case. Some people on the jury . . . had their own agendas. They would not convict under any circumstances."[44] The sentence was six months in prison, a $5,000 fine, and an additional $9,653 fine, which would cover the cost of prison and monthly supervision.

* * * * *

On November 6, 1990, a new era in Washington politics began. Washingtonians chose to demonstrate their growing political maturity by electing as their next mayor, Sharon Pratt Dixon, who promised to lead the city into a responsible future. Without a doubt, reform and change will not come easily. Washington remains the heart of the nation and, as such, the focus all the various political currents and trends.

As Washington moves into its third century, the forecast is bright. Regardless of problems, Washington will survive as one of the world's great cities and the center of political thought for the free world. Perhaps in 100 years, a new author will write, *Three Hundred Years*, which will look back at three centuries of Washington history from a new perspective. In the process, today's heroes may become villains, and likewise, today's villains may become tomorrow's "fascinating historical characters" or even heroes in their own right. Reputations may come and go, but Washington, D.C. will be forever.

Notes

Developing the Dream City

1. Froncek, Thomas, *The City of Washington* (New York: Alfred A. Knopf, 1981), p. 47.
2. (Froncek), p. 35.
3. (Froncek), p. 49.
4. (Forneck), p. 87.
5. (Forncek), p. 87.
6. (Froncek), p. 73.
7. Hutchins, Stilson, *The National Capital* (Washington, D.C.: The Post Publishing Company, 1885), p. 42.
8. Poore, Ben: Perley, *Perley's Reminiscences* (Phildelphia: Hubbard Brothers Publishers, 1886), pp. 53-54.
9. Moore, Joseph West, *Picturesque Washington* (Cedar Rapids, Iowa: G.W. Lyon, Publisher, 1889), p. 30.
10. Hines, Christian, *Washington City* (Washington, D.C.: 1866, reprinted by the Junior League of Washington, 1981), p. 50.
11. (Moore), p. 31.
12. (Hutchins), p. 42.
13. Hardy, Sheila, *A Dying Art* (unpublished manuscript).
14. Kite, Elizabeth S., *L'Enfant and Washington* (Baltimore: The Johns Hopkins Press, 1929), p. 4.
15. (Kite), p. 4.
16. (Kite), p. 14.
17. (Kite), p. 17.
18. (Kite), p. 18.
19. (Froncek), p. 250.
20. (Kite), p. 19
21. (Kite), p. 20
22. (Kite), pp. 85-86.
23. Proctor, John Clagett, *Washington Past and Present* (New York: Lewis Historical Publishing Company, Inc., 1930), p. 547.
24. Bryant, Wilhelmus Bogart, *A History of the National Capital* (New York: The MacMillan Company, 1914), Vol. I, p. 174.
25. Proctor, John Clagett, *Proctor's Washington and Environs* (Washington: written for *The Washington Sunday Star*, 1928-49), p. 45
26. (Proctor, *Proctor's Washington*), p. 45.
27. (Proctor, *Proctor's Washington*), p. 46.
28. (Froncek), p. 50.
29. (Froncek), p. 117.
30. (Hutchins), p. 44.
31. Forbes-Lindsay, C.H., *Washington the City and the Seat of Government* (Philadelphia: The John C. Winston Company, 1908), p. 90.
32. (Bryant), p. 164.
33. (Hutchins), p. 44.
34. (Froncek), p. 62-63.
35. Brown, George Rothwell, *Washington: A Not Too Serious History* (Baltimore: The Norman Publishing Co., 1930), p.22.
36. (Bryant), p. 194.
37. (Bryant), p. 227.
38. (Bryant), p. 283.
39. (Bryant), p. 227.
40. (Bryant), p. 227.
41. (Bryant), p. 254.
42. (Bryant), p. 255.
43. (Bryant), p. 197.
44. (Bryant), p. 198.
45. (Bryant), p. 197.
46. Reiff, Daniel D., *Washington Architecture 1791-1861* (Washington, D.C.: U.S. Commission of Fine Arts, 1971), p. 21.
47. (Froncek), p. 117.
48. (Froncek), p. 68.
49. (Bryant), p. 376.
50. (Bryant), p. 370.
51. (Bryant), p. 370.
52. (Froncek), p. 80.
53. Smith, Margaret Bayard, *The First Forty Years of Washington Society* (New York: Frederick Ungar Publishing Co., 1906), p.58.
54. Wilson, Rufus Rockwell, *Washington the Capital City* (Philadelphia: J.B. Lippincott Co., 1902), p. 103.
55. Green, Constance McLaughlin, *Washington: A History of the Capital, 1800-1950* (Princeton, NJ: Princeton University Press, 1962), Vol. I, p. 57.
56. (Wilson), pp. 142-44.
57. (Smith), p. 380.
58. *Dolly Madison House* (Lompoc, California: Federal Prison Industries, Inc.), p. 4.
59. (Wilson), p. 105.
60. (Wilson), p. 105.

Washington Becomes a Showplace

1. (Bryant), Vol. II, p. 211.
2. (Bryant), Vol. II, p. 241.
3. Exton, Peter and Kleitz, Dorsey, *Milestones into Headstones* (McLean, Virginia: EPM Publications, Inc., 1985), p. 196.
4. (Bryant), p. 232.
5. (Green), Vol. I, p. 104.
6. (Poore), p. 106.
7. (Exton), p. 198.
8. Nicolay, Helen, *Our Capital of the Potomac* (New York: The Century Co., 1924), pp. 306-7.
9. (Exton), p. 197.
10. (Nicolay), p. 221.
11. (Proctor, *Proctor's Washington*), p. 317.
12. Ecker, Grace Dunlop, *A Portrait of Old Georgetown* (Richmond, VA: Garrett & Massie, Inc., 1933), p. 245.
13. (Ecker), p. 246.
14. (Ecker), p. 167.
15. (Ecker), p. 71.
16. (Nicolay), p. 235.
17. (Proctor, *(Proctor's Washington)*), p. 317.
18. Hurd, Charles, *Washington Cavalcade*, (New York: E.P. Dutton & Co. Inc.), p. 72
19. (Smith), p. 252.
20. (Smith), p. 252.
21. (Smith), p. 318.
22. Carr, Roland T., *32 President's Square* (Washington, D.C.: Acropolis Books, Ltd., 1980), p. 79.
23. (Carr), p. 118.
24. (Carr), p. 119.
25. (Carr), p. 202.
26. Kohler, Sue A., and Carson, Jeffrey R., *Sixteenth Street Architecture* (Washington, D.C.: U.S. Government Printing Office), p. 36.
27. *The Washington Post*, February 24, 1990, p. C9.
28. (Exton), p. 185.
29. (Exton), p. 187.
30. Hinkel, John V., *Arlington Monument to Heroes* (Englewood Cliffs, NJ: Prentice-Hall, Inc., 1965), p. 21.
31. (Froncek), p. 169.
32. Crowdrey, Albert E., *A City for the Nation* (Washington, D.C.: U.S. Government Printing Office, 1978), p. 17.
33. (Crowdrey), p. 17.
34. (Crowdrey), p. 17.
35. (Crowdrey), p. 17.
36. (Wilson), p. 208.
37. *The Washington Post*, October 24, 1985.
38. Records of the Columbia Historical Society, Vol. 69-70, pp. 266-305.
39. (Froncek), p. 260.
40. (Froncek). p. 260.
41. Peters, James Edward, *Arlington National Cemetery* (Washington, D.C.: Woodbine House, 1986), p. 25
42. Murdock, Myrtle Cheney, *Constantino Brumidi* (Washington, D.C.: Monumental Press, Inc., 1950), p. 6.
43. (Murdock), p. 14.
44. (Murdock), p. 6.
45. (Murdock), pp. 13-14.
46. (Murdock), pp. 28-29.
47. (Murdock), p. 30.
48. (Murdock), p. 39.
49. (Murdock), p. 16.
50. (Murdock), p. 76.
51. (Murdock), p. 78.
52. (Murdock), p. 7.
53. (Murdock), p. 8.
54. (Murdock), p. 8.

A New Era

1. (Froncek), p. 235.
2. (Green), Vol. I, p. 316.
3. Small, Herbert, *Handbook of the New Library of Congress* (Boston: Curtis & Cameron, 1899), p. 128.
4. (Hurd), p. 132.
5. (Hutchins), p. 68.
6. (Moore), p. 50.
7. (Moore), p. 50.
8. (Green), Vol. I, p. 349.
9. (Green), Vol. I, p. 350.
10. (Green), Vol., p. 360.
11. (Bryant), p. 633.
12. (Green), Vol. II, p. 81.
13. (Green), p. 101.
14. Douglass, Frederick, *Narrative* (New York: Signet, 1968), p. 22.
15. (Douglass), p. 44.
16. (Douglass), p. 49.
17. (Douglass), p. 92-3.
18. (Douglass), p. 111.
19. (Douglass), p. 112.
20. (Douglass), p. 112.
21. (Douglass), p. 116.
22. (Douglass), p. 119.

23. Lewis, David L., *District of Columbia A History* (New York: W.W. Norton & Co, Inc., 1976), p. 63.

24. Lee, Richard M., *Mr. Lincoln's City* (McLean, VA: EPM Publications, Inc., 1981), p. 128.

25. Records of the Columbia Historical Society, Vol. 50th, p. 361.

26. (Green), Vol. I, p. 370.

27. (Green), Vol. II, p. 117.

28. Carpenter, Frank G., *Carp's Washington* (New York: McGraw-Hill Book Company, Inc., 1960), p. 243.

29. Hutchinson, Louise Daniel, *The Anacostia Story* (Washington, D.C.: Smithsonian Press, 1977), p. 108.

30. (Hutchinson), p. 108.

31. (Hutchinson), p. 108.

32. *Washington Times-Herald*, June 6, 1940, p. C3.

33. *The Washingtonian*, July 1979, p. 119.

34. (*The Washingtonian*), p. 125.

35. (*The Washingtonian*), p. 122.

36. *The Washington Post*, April 29, 1943.

37. *The Washington Post*, April 29, 1943.

38. *The Washington Post*, April 29, 1943.

39. *The Evening Star*, November 12, 1950.

40. *The Evening Star*, November 12, 1950.

41. *The Evening Star*, November 12, 1950.

42. *The Evening Star*, November 12, 1950.

43. *The Evening Star*, November 12, 1950.

44. *The Evening Star*, November 12, 1950.

45. *The Evening Star*, November 12, 1950.

46. *The Evening Star*, November 12, 1950.

47. *The Evening Star*, November 12, 1950.

48. *The Evening Star*, November 12, 1950.

49. *The Times-Herald*, February 6, 1936.

50. Eskew, Garnett Laidlaw, *Willard's of Washington* (New York: Coward-McCann, Inc., 1950), p. 108.

51. (Eskew), p. 20.

52. (Eskew), p. 127.

53. (Eskew), p. 99.

54. (Eskew), p. 73.

55. (Eskew), p, 194.

36. *The Evening Star*, 1989.

Culture, Money, Depression, and War

1. *The Washingtonian*, April 1984, p. 174.

2. Kohler, Sue A., and Carson, Jeffrey R., *Sixteenth Street Architecture, Volume 2* (Washington, D.C.: U.S. Government Printing Office, 1988), p. 20.

3. *The Washingtonian*, April 1984, p. 174.

4. (Kohler), Vol. 2, p. 21.

5. (Kohler), Vol. 2, p. 22.

6. *The Washingtonian*, April 1984, p. 175.

7. (Kohler), Vol. 2, p. 23.

8. (Kohler), Vol. 2, p. 23.

9. (Kohler), Vol. 2, p. 23.

10. (Kohler), Vol. 2, p. 24.

11. Goode, James M., *Best Addresses* (Washington, D.C.: Smithsonian Press, 1988), p. 180.

12. *The Washingtonian*, October 1989, p. 153.

13. *Museum Washington*, June/July 1986, p. 8.

14. *Men of the Rebellion* (Washington, D.C.: The Phillips Collection, 1990), p. 12.

15. *The Washingtonian*, October 1989, p. 154.

16. (*Museum Washington*), p. 8.

17. (Men of the Rebellion), p. 6.

18. (*Museum Washington*), p. 9.

19. *The Washington Post*, June 15, 1986, p. B10.

20. (*Men of the Rebellion*), p. 25.

21. *The Washington Post*, June 15, 1986, p. B10.

22. Felsenthal, Carol, *Alice Roosevelt Longworth* (New York: G.P. Putnam's Sons, 1988), p. 64.

23. (Felsenthal), p. 67.

24. (Felsenthal), p. 68.

25. (Felsenthal), p. 117.

26. *Boudoir Mirrors of Washington* (Philadelphia: The John C. Winston Co., 1923), p. 17.

27. (Felsenthal), p. 146.

28. (Felsenthal), p. 123.

29. (Felsenthal), p. 167.

30. (Felsenthal), p. 175.

31. (Felsenthal), p. 255.

32. (Felsenthal), p. 259.

33. (Felsenthal), p. 247.

34. (Felsenthal), p. 269.

35. (Felsenthal), p. 66.

36. Martin, Ralph G., *Cissy* (New York: Simon and Schuster, 1979), p. 47.

37. (Martin), p. 51.

38. (Martin), p. 104.

39. (Martin), p. 244.

40. (Martin), p. 271.

41. (Martin), p. 427.

42. (Martin), p. 400.

43. (Martin), p. 475.

44. *The Washingtonian*, April 1979, p. 90.

45. *The Washingtonian*, April 1979, p. 92.

46. *The Washington Times-Herald*, November 10, 1930.
47. *The Washington Times-Herald*, November 13, 1930.
48. *The Washington Times-Herald*, November 13, 1930.
49. *The Washingtonian*, April 1979, p. 94.
50. (Lewis), p. 113.
51. *The Washington Post*, April 29, 1989.
52. *The Washingtonian*, May 1989, p. 98.
53. *The Washingtonian*, May 1989, p. 105.
54. *The Washingtonian*, May 1982, p. 112.
55. *The Washingtonian*, May 1989, p. 102.
56. *Washington Afro-American*, March 8, 1983.
57. *The New York Review*, November 19, 1987, p. 3.
58. (*The New York Review*), p. 4.
59. (*The New York Review*), p. 4.
60. *The Washington Post*, December 19, 1985.
61. *The Washington Post*, April 18, 1986.
62. (*Washington Afro-American*)
63. *The Washington Post*, April 29, 1989.

The World's Capital

1. *The Washingtonian*, April 1984, p. 116.
2. *The Washingtonian*, April 1984, p. 116.
3. *The Washingtonian*, April 1984, p. 116.
4. *The Washingtonian*, April 1984, p. 165.
5. *The Washingtonian*, April 1984, p. 168.
6. *The Washingtonian*, April 1984, p. 165.
7. *The Washingtonian*, April 1984, p. 117.
8. *The Washingtonian*, April 1984, p. 117.
9. *The Washington Post Magazine*, February 25, 1990, p. 33.
10. *The Washington Post Magazine*, February 15, 1990, p. 20.
11. Roberts, Chalmers M., *The Washington Post, The First 100 Years* (Boston: Houghton Mifflin Co., 1977), pp. 366-68.
12. (Roberts), p. 368.
13. (Roberts), p. 369.
14. (Roberts), p. 369.
15. (Roberts), p. 369.
16. *The Washingtonian*, December 1985, p. 131.
17. *The Washingtonian*, December 1985, p. 185.
18. (Roberts), p. 371.
19. *The Washingtonian*, December 1985, p. 185.
20. *The Washingtonian*, December 1985, p. 185.
21. *The Washingtonian*, December 1985, p. 188.
22. *The Washingtonian*, December 1985, p. 204.
23. *The Washingtonian*, December 1985, p. 213.
24. Schott, Joseph L., *No Left Turns* (New York: Praeger Publishers, 1975), p. 113.
25. (Schott), p. 110.
26. Falb, Susan Rosenfeld, *History of the J. Edgar Hoover Building* (Washington, D.C.: Office of Congressional and Public Affairs, U.S. Department of Justice, 1987), p.2.
27. *The Washington Post*, December 30, 1966.
28. *The Washington Post*, November 13, 1955.
29. *The Washington Post*, "Helen Hayes: A Career Is Ending."
30. *The Washington Post*, November 13, 1955.
31. *The Washington Post*, November 13, 1955.
32. *The Washington Post*, December 12, 1935.
33. *The Washington Daily News*, December 20, 1955.
34. *The Evening Star*, November 9, 1955.
35. *The Washington Post*, November 13, 1955.
36. *The Washington Post*, June 6, 1971.
37. *The Washington Post Magazine*, April 26, 1987, p. 23.
38. *The Washingtonian*, December 1984, p. 180.
39. *The Washingtonian*, December 1984, p. 175.
40. *The Washington Post*, Tony Kornheiser, June 1, 1990.
41. *The Washington Post*, Tony Kornheiser, June 1, 1990.
42. *The Washington Post Magazine*, May 20, 1990, p. 9.
13. *The Washington Post*, Tony Kornheiser, June 1, 1990.
44. *The Washington Post*, October 31, 1990, p. A1.

Index